I0815849

WHAT PEOPLE ARE SAYING ABOUT

LIVING A CHARMED LIFE

"*Living a Charmed Life* is the heart-wrenching yet inspirational story of how Linda Blue dealt with broken relationships, the repeated loss of family members, and the general confusions and frustrations of life and yet found in all that tragedy the message that she must work to enjoy her life every day to the point where she has come to believe it is charmed. You'll never forget this book, and you'll come away grateful for all the blessings you experience."

— Patrick Snow, Publishing Coach and Bestselling Author of *Creating Your Own Destiny* and *The Affluent Entrepreneur*

"It's hard to imagine anyone whose life has been less charmed than Linda Blue's, and yet despite all the loss and tragedy in her life, she has found a way to believe she is living a charmed life. You will not believe what she has gone through, and you will rejoice that she has been able to stay positive and write this book that shows no matter what we go through, we can handle it and still find the charm in all around us."

— Tyler R. Tichelaar, PhD and Award-Winning Author of *Narrow Lives* and *The Best Place*

"Amid tragedy, heartbreak, and all life's obstacles, Linda Blue reveals that we can all live a charmed life if we just look at the good all around us. Linda writes truthfully about her experiences with loss and love and how those fueled her desire to live her life fully, refusing to give up on life and love until the very end. Insightful, truthful, tear-packed, and energy-packed, *Living a Charmed Life* will keep you engrossed until the very end."

— Nicole Gabriel, Author of *Finding Your Inner Truth*
and *Stepping Into Your Becoming*

"Linda has written a fascinating and moving memoir about hope and happiness even in the wake of life's deepest tragedies. *Living a Charmed Life* tracks Linda's journey from despair to hope and gratitude as well as the lessons she learned along the way. I would urge anyone who has been touched by the loss of a loved one to read this book. Linda shows you that it is possible to navigate through emotional and physical losses and come out on the other side of grief stronger than before."

— Jennifer R. Newell, Owner and Creative
Director of SB Creative Content

LIVING A CHARMED LIFE

HOW TO FEEL AND DEAL TO HEAL

LINDA ALLEN BLUE

LIVING A CHARMED LIFE:
How to Feel and Deal to Heal

Copyright © 2024 by Linda Allen Blue. All rights reserved.

Published by:
Aviva Publishing
Lake Placid, NY 12946
518-523-1320
www.avivapubs.com

All Rights Reserved. No part of this book may be used or reproduced in any manner whatsoever without the expressed written permission of the author.

Address all inquiries to:
Linda Allen Blue
PO Box 90653
Santa Barbara, CA 93190
(805) 708-2583
www.LindaAllenBlue.com

ISBN: 978-1-63618-317-6

Library of Congress Control Number: 2024901761

Editor: Tyler Tichelaar, Superior Book Productions
Cover Design and Interior Layout: Nicole Gabriel, Let's Get Your Book Published
Author Photo Credit: T. Watkins

Every attempt has been made to properly source all quotes.

Printed in the United States of America

First Edition

2 4 6 8 10 12

This book is dedicated to my family.
Through their suffering came enlightenment.

ACKNOWLEDGMENTS

Of course, my family and friends are at the top of my list to thank, but several people whom I consider my chosen family always had their hearts and doors open to me when I was going through some of the most challenging times in my life. Sam and Steve, thank you from the bottom of my heart for your unrelenting, humorous, and unconditional love. Ari and Brian, my gratitude to you is endless for getting me through an extremely stressful time, and I cannot thank you enough for your selfless love and support. Joe, you were my rock in getting me through the three worst years in my life; I am eternally grateful. Leslie, you showed up for me when I sat alone at the hospital waiting for ten hours. And for every funeral, you pulled your kids out of school, teaching them how to support a friend grieving the loss of her family. I am so grateful you are my friend. And for the friends who lost sisters, fathers, and mothers before me, thank you for sharing your experiences of loss with me. You showed me that life does go on after death….

CONTENTS

INTRODUCTION

I've been writing this book for more than fifteen years. Reading some of the chapters have made me cry, even weep. I can't even believe this is my life story. It is mind-blowing. My intent is for this book to help someone who is having a hard time. My hope is to help others find the silver lining in the dark clouds that can loom in life. I have written this book in the rawest form. The thoughts are my own. I certainly own them. I can't hide, fight, or suppress them. They are mine. I invite you to be inspired by them. That is the only reason I have turned my personal journals into this book. That's it. I'm not looking for sympathy or criticism. I'm just living my life and trying to find happiness along the way. I hope my story will help you to do the same.

Linda Blue

MY LIFE IN A NUTSHELL

When I was a child, if anyone would have told me this would be my life, I would have looked at them and run away as fast as I could. But at this point in my life, all I can do is look at it all as a learning experience. Life is a journey, not a destination. All I can figure is I am here to learn from this journey rather than wish for a better life because without my lessons, I wouldn't be the person I am, and I would look at life so very differently. Sometimes, I actually feel lucky to have learned some of the lessons so early in my life. They have helped me put the little things into perspective. I want to give you an overview of the major events in my life in this chapter so the individual chapters in the rest of this book will have better context for you.

I guess I should start at the beginning; that would be 1967 when I was born and raised in Huntington Beach, California. I was born to an alcoholic father and a codependent mother. I am the youngest of four. My siblings are six, seven, and eight years older than me. I often wonder what my mother was thinking, but back then, there was no birth control for good Catholic women. That came after me.

Some of my earliest memories are not the wonderful kind. They are the kind I don't know what to do with sometimes. One time, when I was pretty young, I was woken in the middle of the night by my mom and sisters yelling and pleading with my dad to leave my brother Bobby (the only son) alone. I could hear someone getting hit in my brother's room. My dad had come home drunk and in a terrible mood, gone up to my brother's room, woken him, and started in on him. And my family wonders why we have issues. Another memory is being woken out of a sound sleep and rushed off to the camper, then waking in some strange neighborhood. Oddly, I don't remember thinking it was unusual; it was normalcy in my home.

On another occasion (of many), my sister Karen escaped our home's alcoholic chaos through the second-story window; she scaled down to the ground and ran to our friends, who were also alcoholics, in the next track of homes for help. I guess she knew they'd understand. I suppose calling the police would have caused a lot more trouble! We would leave in a hurry with the dogs in tow and go to the drive-in theater to hide. Another time, my dad dismantled the car before he came into the house so we couldn't leave. That's just a taste of the lovely and peaceful home I was raised in. Not too long after, my mom filed for divorce for obvious reasons. But Dad cried and begged and made her believe he'd change. She went back, and until their deaths, they remained married.

High school started off great. The summer before my freshman year, I lost ten pounds doing Junior Lifeguards, which gave me confidence. I felt good about myself. My sophomore year, I was probably hormonal and felt suicidal. I just didn't want to live. I imagined killing myself with pills or some other way, but I imagined my mom finding me, and I just couldn't do that to her. At church, I told my friends what I wanted to do. They looked at me with concern, but I didn't think they took me seriously. The next day at school, I was called into the Campus Youth Ministry office. I was asked if I knew why they had called me in. I said no. They said my friends had told them they were worried I was going to kill myself. In that moment, I knew my friends loved me and didn't want a tragic ending to my life. I never threatened to kill myself again. It was a wake-up lesson that has stayed with me forever. I am eternally grateful for their concern. The rest of high school was fun, and I never looked back.

I went on to a junior college and took a summer session class in photography. I had received a camera for graduation but had no idea how to use it. There were all these buttons and numbers and things I didn't recognize, and I had no idea what they meant, so I thought I should figure it out and enrolled in Photography 101. I loved every minute of it. I learned how to print black-and-white photos and spent hours in the dark room. One day, I was there for eight hours and came out feeling happy. I didn't even think of making photography my career, but I showed my friends Julie and Stephanie the images I had created. They both said my images were really good and I should do something with my talent. After that, I looked into schools and found Brooks Institute of Photography in Santa Barbara. I applied and was accepted.

In 1988, I had my first experience with death. Grandma Lottie, my mom's mother, died. She had diabetes, which ultimately took her life. She was such a good lady, and she was all the good in our family (I like to say that all the good in me comes from my mom's side of the family and all the naughty comes from my dad's side.) I was the last one to see her alive. I left the hospital after telling her she would get better. She simply shook her head and said, "No." The doctor had told her they needed to remove her lower leg, but she wanted nothing to do with it. A little while after I got home, the hospital called to say she had passed. We were shocked. My heart wept for my mom because she had loved her mother so much. We all had. This was my first experience figuring out how to handle grief.

Later that year, I went off to college. I absolutely loved Santa Barbara and would live there for twenty-eight years. Had my friends not told me I was good, I would have never pursued photography as a career.

When I was still in college, in 1990, my sister Karen was diagnosed with leukemia. I was her bone marrow donor. My sisters Gayle and Karen and I all matched in blood type, but I was a better choice because Gayle had a childhood disease I had not had. Watching Karen fight cancer was humbling and horrible. I felt numb through most of it. Her son Travis was just four at the time. He wasn't allowed in her hospital room, so he had to see her through the window. He didn't understand why he couldn't hug his mom. It was heartbreaking to watch. We all put on our brave faces, showing him that it was okay. We really didn't know how it was all going to work out—live or die. Karen was in the hospital for two months. All that time, I felt like I was holding my breath and asking God to please leave her on earth for a while longer. She survived and began to thrive again, but City of Hope—the hospital she was at—told her that with all the chemo and radiation they had put into her body, she would get cancer again in about ten years. In eleven years, she got colon cancer and uterine cancer. We thought the diagnosis was a blessing because when they were removing her uterine cancer, they found more colon cancer and were able to get it out. When they removed her colon cancer, they gave her a J Pouch instead of colostomy bag. This allowed her to go on and live a normal life until it started getting blocked. This was truly painful for her, and each time it happened, she was unable to eat for a week. She got a little weaker and lost weight each time.

Meanwhile, I was at school, and there I met Billy. I thought marriage was the next natural step in life, so after I graduated, we tied the knot. I found out that was not a good reason to get married, and five-and-a-half-years later, we divorced. It was a tumultuous marriage, and it cured me of a next marriage. I never wanted to get married again because I had felt so trapped.

The same year we got married, in 1993, Grandpa Louie died. He was a sweet man who had an interesting past. He was a jeweler who lost all of his money gambling—he lost everything! He was Al Capone's personal jeweler, and when he left Chicago, he became the first jeweler in Huntington Beach, California. After Grandma Lottie's first husband died in his twenties of heart disease, she met Louie and they married. Grandpa Louie adopted my mom and they were all happy.

Two months after Grandpa Louie died, my sister Gayle was diagnosed with brain cancer. She was feeling off balance and went to the doctor. The very next day, at 8 a.m., she had brain surgery. She was never the same again. She lost her short-term memory and became an invalid. That broke our hearts a little more after a pretty messed up year. My mom questioned God on this one. Now two of her daughters had cancer. She was a devout Catholic, so when she began to question God, I didn't know what to think. It was a sad time in our lives, and we didn't know how it would pan out. After the surgery, the doctor told us if they removed any more of the walnut-size tumor, it would compromise her brain. I hate to think how she could have been any more compromised than she was! The doctor told my brother-in-law Dan that if they didn't perform the surgery, she would live six months, but with it, she would live eighteen months. Boy, was that doctor wrong! She went on to live sixteen-and-a-half years in a completely fucked-up and debilitated state! Her kids lost their mother when she was just thirty-four. Even though she was physically alive, she couldn't think cognitively or raise her family anymore. We missed her, even though we could see her. It was just sad to witness, and our hearts broke a little more when it became clear that this state would be the rest of her life.

That same year, my dad retired from being a pilot for thirty years. I could have gone on his last flight, but I didn't because I was in another place with my new marriage and now my other sister also had cancer. It was all new territory I had to figure out how to navigate. Years later, I was coming back from a trip when the pilot announced it was his last flight and he was retiring. I lost it and started crying; I knew in that moment I had made a huge mistake by not going on my dad's last flight. I could hardly contain my tears and sobbed quietly in my seat.

Life was moving along. Though getting divorced was hard, I managed to get back up. I met the love of my life in 2000. Jim was a charismatic man and I was smitten! We stayed together for seven years. A year after Jim and I broke up, I met Joe and we went out for five years, on and off until 2013.

Hopefully, all this background information will help the individual chapters about my life make more sense when you read them. I started writing the journal entries in 2002 and they run through the year 2023. Some of the events I record are happy, some are sad, and some broke my heart....

PART I

FAILING RELATIONSHIPS

1

Dad

Let's start at the root of my issues—my dad. I'm not sure I'm ready to start with him, but here it goes. He's actually a very smart man. He can do just about anything. He can build a house, install electricity and plumbing, rebuild a car engine, do metal plating and finishing, fly airplanes, weld, make replica gun boxes from the 1800s, etc. He is a wealth of knowledge in any area he sets out to learn about. But nobody raised him emotionally.

I still struggle with our relationship. I got into a physical fight with him on the front lawn when I was twenty, which today he finds amusing. I began understanding him in my mid-twenties. After listening to him argue with my nephew, who was eight at the time, I couldn't tell which one was eight! That is when I found out where he came from. His real father, Jack, met my grandma Lill and married her after knowing her a very short time. When she got pregnant, he left her. He ended up bootlegging for Al Capone and dying an alcoholic in his forties.

My dad told me a couple of stories about his father from when my dad was a young boy. One time, my grandma took my dad to see his father and try to get some child support. At the time, Jack worked in a meat-packing place, not making ends meat! Just kidding. Anyhow, Jack refused the poor mother and son, and on their way out, Jack threw a hunk of meat at my grandma, hitting her in the back of the head! That is one of my dad's few memories about his father; needless to say, his father was not a very good role model. The only other story my dad told me about Grandpa Jack is from when he was dying from alcoholism. He begged my dad to bury him in a real plot, not in the potter's field where all the people without money or loved ones got buried. Well, my dad was only seventeen and had no money, so when Jack died, he was buried in the potter's field. Sad story.

After learning this information from my dad and seeing him argue with my eight-year-old nephew, I understood that nobody had raised him emotionally. Grandma Lill was a single parent, so she wasn't around much, between working and trying to find a new husband. Perhaps that all kept her from properly raising her son.

2

My Brother-in-Law Jim

"You always make me feel better when I talk to you." Those were some of the last words I remember my brother-in-law Jim saying to me before he took his life. A lot of things have gone through my mind since he committed suicide on October 27, 2002. When someone kills themselves, it's not the same as if they died from an accident or disease. There are different questions I can't help but ask myself: "Why didn't I call him just to see how he was doing?" or "How could I not have known how sad, lonely, and desperate he was?" What I have the most difficulty with is how truly sad this human being was to do this tragic act. He loved his son and his wife, but he couldn't love himself. He had been struggling for so very long with himself, and my only consoling thoughts are that he is finally at peace. He is now with his mother, who died of cancer.

I met Jim when he and my sister started dating. On Christmas Day, he dropped off a gift for Karen. She ran upstairs to hide and said, "Tell him I'm not here!" He gave her two gifts—a nice, big gym bag and a box of Snarol Snail and Slug Killer. Perhaps his message to my sister was "Stop being a slimy slug!" I found humor in his gift selection. I figured she deserved it, although her gut was telling her to run for some reason. Anyway, they ended up together and were married a few years later.

Jim's drug and alcohol abuse was not a big secret even to the "little" sister. They always tried to hide the big stuff from me, but I could handle it. Maybe if they had shared a little more with me, I might not have married an addict myself.

Recently, Karen told me why she ran from Jim. She knew he had deep-seated issues. But he kept pursuing her and she found it flattering. I wonder what life would be like now if he had never won her over. I also wonder whether Jim never really got over his mom's death or Karen's cancer. I can't help but wonder if he would still be alive if he had chosen to deal with death, sadness, and grief in a healthier way, rather than leaning on his addictions.

I wrote the following poem about him:

Emptiness

No one really knows the emptiness he felt inside
The anguish

The sadness
The loneliness.
Though not one of us could ever fix this, we all wished we had tried.
His depression couldn't be fixed with his addictions.
His emptiness made him lose his ambitions.
I truly believe he is at peace finally
Something he could never find on this earth.
A troubled man for so long
Never felt he belonged.
As hard as he tried, he couldn't seem to succeed in happiness.
He had a restless soul
And a giving heart.
He worked hard
And played as hard as he worked.
All work is done now, rest in peace.

3

Unbearable

Some days, I find the pain I feel here on this earth unbearable. I just feel weepy from thinking about losing a loved one to suicide. I find it hard to just get on with life. Most days are okay until I start thinking about Jim and how I'll never see him again. It's so final. Taking your own life is just so hard for the rest of us. I suppose this is part of healing, but it never feels like there's anything I can do to fix how it makes me feel. I can't imagine what Jim's father must be going through. There was alcoholism and mental illness in Jim's family when he was growing up. I would think it might make a father second-guess his actions in raising his son. I think Jim always wanted to feel and appreciate the little things in life, and maybe, he just couldn't figure it out on his own. His family seems unemotional to me. Maybe they're just being brave and know how to hide their feelings better than I do.

Today is Jim's birthday. I feel somber. I think most about his son, Travis. He's trying to move on with his life and is socializing with his friends. At fifteen, how can he even grasp the heaviness of suicide? He didn't even want his friends to know his dad had died. He especially didn't want them to know he took his own life. I wonder what effect it will have on Travis. After all, growing up in an alcoholic and codependent environment is all too familiar to me. I wonder what I would be like if my dad had killed himself when I was fifteen. When I was that age, my dad was diagnosed with bladder cancer. I don't recall feeling back then. Maybe for Travis it was a relief. The vicious cycle could finally come to an end, at least with his father. If he doesn't choose to deal with it all at some point, he will have the same kinds of codependent relationships with others that he had with Jim. Perhaps, after a few unhealthy relationships, he'll figure out that it's time to look inside himself.

4

Acceptance

Today I learned acceptance. I'm still not sure if that's a good thing. My mom was just diagnosed with a cancerous, grade three brain tumor. She was told that without treatment, she has six months to live. Those are some pretty harsh words to hear, but the words "It's treatable" were the next to be said. I'm hanging on to "treatable," and I won't let go. I can think of nothing else right now, but to accept this as our fate.

I can't believe this is the second brain tumor in my immediate family. I never imagined it could come again. I keep thinking it was the second-hand smoke that caused this too. Karen wants to fight, blame something or somebody, but I accept. At this point, I can't do anything to stop this horrible disease. But I refuse to let it make me miserable and sad for the rest of my life. I don't think that's the point, or what I'm supposed to take from it. It does make me sad if I let it, but I believe it's important to laugh as hard as I can, to love as much as my heart can, and to live my life as if I won't always get tomorrow.

This has been a lot for one family to endure, and I can't help but wonder why. What am I supposed to get out of this? What is it I'm supposed to figure out in this lifetime? I can't answer those questions all at once, but each day, I learn something new about me. Some days, I learn something new about others, but I'm more concerned with how I can be a better human being. I've decided that when people behave badly, or "ugly on the inside" as I like to call it, it comes from their insecurities and fears. I haven't yet met anyone who doesn't have fears and insecurities. As hard as I try, I still meet my demons all the time, but I try to make amends or sincerely apologize if I have wronged someone. Sometimes they never speak to me again, and that's hard for me to accept, but I know I have to let them go.

5

The Owl

Today, November 12, 2002, is my thirty-fifth birthday. I just got home from my birthday celebration with friends. I entered my home with no expectations, and I got the most beautiful wishes I've ever received. Words like, "You make the room brighter when you come in." They completely blow my mind and touch my heart. I never thought in a million years, that I, of all the people, am capable of touching someone in such a way. There was a bouquet of balloons, and a bag of kisses, and a present. It almost hurt like a broken heart, but in a positive way. The emotions seem to be the same, and I'm so touched. I guess I can't believe that after all the crap I've been through, I have actually figured out a few things along the way. I've found out how to love and how to find the good in the difficulties that come. I find that people really appreciate that, and they find inspiration along the way. It's actually okay to go on with your life when someone else leaves this earth.

One of my guardian angels was out tonight. He was a homeless man. But, somehow I knew he was there for me. He spoke clearly and soberly, and I just *knew* he had something to say to me. I can't explain it, or why I felt this way, but I just knew. I asked him something specific, and he said that my brother-in-law had gone on to his next life. Jim wasn't at peace, but trying to figure out his soul for his next life. Then he rambled out some biblical names. Then the manager of the restaurant asked him to leave. I got the gist; it was what I had already suspected. Odd how I need a stranger to confirm my belief, which I don't even know how I got, to move on. Oh, and how did I even know this person would be the one to reassure me anyway? I guess I had some strange feeling that *he* would be out tonight.

As soon as I arrived home, my dog Rufus had her needs too! So we went outside just like any other morning, noon, or night. As we entered the calm dark night, something was different. A new sound could be heard. It was a wonderful sound—one I don't hear very often. It was an owl. It was wonderful! It reassured me that I am in the right place. It's call has such a different ring to it. I felt so right at this time. I heard it a few more times as I wrote this, and then he was gone.

6

Trusting My Gut

When I was in my early twenties, I knew I should know a man at least five years before deciding to marry him. I'm not sure where I got that idea, but I believed in it. Then, for some reason, in my mid-twenties, that knowledge went out of my head and I married when I was twenty-five. I guess I didn't trust my gut because after leaving my marriage, I remembered the five-year rule. I did the math of how long I had been in my relationship, and lo and behold, I had known him five years when I knew I needed to leave my marriage. I stayed a bit longer, but it was five years (almost to the month) when I realized I was very unhappy and didn't want to spend the rest of my life that way. I knew it was time to move on.

Once I was out of my relationship, I started paying more attention to my inner voice. Boy, was it talking! I couldn't believe some of the things that would just come out of my mouth! One of my roommates was befriending an older family man. He was friends with her father, so she thought it was okay. I didn't like something about this man, but I couldn't quite tell what it was. One day, my roommate told me she was going to dinner with him. Without thinking, I said, "You better watch out; he might ask you for a blowjob!" She was offended, and I apologized, but I still told her to be careful. Nothing happened that night, but a week later, I came home to a house full of cops, a hysterical roommate, and one very suspicious-looking man standing on the sidewalk. As the story unfolded, I couldn't believe what a pig he truly was! He did, in fact, ask her for a blowjob with a fist full of money. Inside my head, I was freaking out! I guess I did know why I didn't like this man.

After that, I knew I needed to listen more carefully to my gut and trust my instincts because they were likely to be right!

7

Mom

I used to think I was supposed to save my mom, but as I became a young adult and was on my own for the first time, I realized only she could save herself. We all make our own choices and decide what is right for us at the time we make them. I don't know why we make wrong choices, but perhaps it's as simple as that's what we are here to learn.

My mom chose to stay in a marriage that was degrading, seemingly hateful, abusive, and so wrong. I just realized if my mom hadn't chosen to stay in her marriage, I might have stayed in mine. Without seeing what could happen if I stayed in an alcoholic relationship, it might not have occurred to me that I could leave—something I always thought my mom should have done. Maybe, in a sense, she sacrificed herself to save her children the misery. Maybe if my parents had divorced, I would have felt the need to stay with my husband at all costs. I don't know. Maybe if my parents had divorced, I never would have married "my father."

My mom is a true caretaker—of everyone except herself. She had four children. At one time, she had a newborn, a one-year-old, and a two-year-old. I know that's how it was back then, but that's still a lot of work! I came six years later, so I was almost like an only child. My siblings were all teenagers by the time I was seven. My dad was of no help at all, which is how it was back then. Even when he was around, he would wreak havoc in his drunken stupors. My mom would always call it a vacation whenever he left on a trip. She would get excited and say to us, "Let's go have some fun, and go to lunch and shop!" That's about all the fun she ever had.

My mom is a devout Catholic. She goes to church every morning and prays for us. She never was a "holy roller" or tried to make me feel guilty for not going with her as an adult. She never preaches at us, only prays for us. She gives and gives and gives. I don't think I've ever heard her ask me for anything except to make my bed.

My mom was very young when her father died of heart disease in his twenties. Her mother had to figure out a way to survive, so she put my mom on the family farm, picking potatoes. My mom only spoke Polish till she was six. Then, Grandma Lottie met Grandpa Louie, and they brought her back to Chicago to live as a family. One of my favorite stories about my mom is when they showed her to her new room. She looked inside the drawers and saw they were full of all new clothes! New slips, dresses, shoes, underwear—anything she could imagine! She squealed with delight! Okay, I made up that squealing part, but I'm sure she was delighted. I can just tell by the way she tells the story that it was one of her fondest childhood memories.

Now, I feel like she might be slipping away. Eighteen months ago, she was diagnosed with a malignant brain tumor. Without any treatment, they gave her six months to live. She opted to have a procedure called Gamma Knife. She absolutely did not want brain surgery, and I do not blame her. After she watched my sister Gayle go through brain surgery and its outcome, it was something she wanted nothing to do with, and I didn't encourage her to change her mind. I would have made the same decision. For a while now, Mom has been doing okay.

8

Change

I had an interesting conversation last night with someone I hardly know. It started with me asking an insecure question. The answer was the most interesting part. "If you don't change, " was the response. *If I don't change?* I thought. *Of course I'm going to change. I will evolve, and if you don't, then you have the problem.* Change is so important to our well-being. If I didn't change, I'd still be the same as I was when I wasn't so pleasant.

I work hard on myself each and every day, and some days are definitely harder than others. I've changed how I take other people's actions, and instead of reacting to them and their sometimes outrageous behavior, I ask myself what could possibly be going on in their life to make them so ugly on the inside? Instead of just thinking about how they made me feel, I take it to a new level. I wonder if everything is okay in their world, and I hope that everything gets better for them or they find their answers. Of course, some days I find it difficult to respond this way, but if I stop myself in mid-thought, I can usually talk myself out of disliking another person for their behavior. Usually, the angry ones have something very wrong going on in their world, and realizing that makes it much easier to walk away from their negative energy.

I find the people closest to me are the hardest ones to respond to in the right way. Maybe that's because I expect more from them. Maybe I shouldn't. My dad is a good example. He loves to push my buttons, and I, in turn, push his right back. It gets pretty ugly, and it usually ends with him yelling at me to get the "blank" out of his house! He doesn't get that when he hits below the belt, I'm gonna come back and make it hurt. I think he has control issues, and he knows he no longer has a hold on me. I'm not his dependent any longer, so he can't hold tuition or any other financial control over me. I think this really bugs him. I've changed my response to his request for me to leave, but I still haven't figured out how to not let him get to me. I think he does get to me because I believe a father shouldn't treat his children this way. I find it disgraceful.

At this point in my life, I don't visit my parents too much anymore. Doing so is too upsetting. Recently, I let my dad know he's the reason I don't go down there anymore. I was crying hysterically. He is the person who affects me in the most emotional way. Wow, that was a revelation! I just try to understand and get along with him. Change is so hard in this area because he won't change or doesn't have the capacity to do it. Nobody taught him. And if they did, he didn't listen.

Only I can change me. I can't change anybody else, and I'm not here to do so. Although, sometimes I try to enlighten others, but not everyone is ready to change, and that's okay. We all have to grow when we are ready to grow. And when we're ready, we'll hear all kinds of things that will help inspire us to change! That's a beautiful thing! Personal growth is one of my favorite things to do! And change goes hand-in-hand with personal growth.

9

Society's Rules

Just because society lives one way doesn't mean that way is for everyone. I feel bad for a friend who thinks because she's thirty-seven and hasn't gotten married or had children—or in this day and age, become divorced with children—she's not living. I think she's smart to be single. Or lucky. She won't even go to her high school reunion because she thinks her peers will think something is wrong with her for not following society's so-called rules of getting married and pregnant at a young age like our parents did.

Nowadays, it's a good thing to decide how to live your life. Not how it was in the 1950s. We have choices now. But I guess being single hasn't been her choice, which makes it a bad thing in her mind. She hasn't gotten married because she hasn't found the right person. I, on the other hand, did get married, and it wasn't the right person. I had a really rough time getting through that experience. Self-doubt, single again, sadness, broken promise. But I had to live through my own experience, just like my friend. The only difference is she is trying to create an experience that has not happened. She is trying to write her own screenplay of her life. I think it's fine to keep looking for the perfect situation, but sometimes, life just happens. I truly believe we meet the people we are supposed to meet, and sometimes they are only temporary. Sometimes, they stay a lifetime.

I got married when I did because it seemed like the next step in life. I didn't really look at who I was with or whether he was a good match for me. I just felt we loved each other, but I didn't look at the relationship dynamics, and we didn't get to know each other long enough. I was young, too young. I also thought having children was the next logical step in life. Then I realized this man I was with was never available. I realized if I had a child, I would be a single parent within my marriage. Instinctively, I knew not to have children at that time.

As our marriage progressed, so did the issues, and they became much bigger. The need to leave the marriage became very clear about two-and-a-half years in. But I was raised as a good Catholic, and being codependent seemed to be a characteristic of a good wife. You know, "for better or for worse." I left during the worse part. I just didn't feel I could stay with the father I was raised by. My father quit drinking for eight years after my mom served him with divorce papers, but eventually, he went back to drinking. I saw that, and I knew my father had quit drinking for the wrong reasons. He quit for everyone except himself. He didn't quit for himself. He quit to keep his woman by his side. She took care of his ass! She did everything for him, including taking every ounce of his degrading insults, which no human should ever be subjected to.

It's so important to face one's past in order to move effectively into one's present. Our issues will always be there, so the only way to begin to delve into fixing them is to face them. I don't like to go back to my childhood very often, but I do know that's where my issues originated. If I can look them in the face, accept them for what they are, and accept myself for who I am, then I have started the battle. I'm all about confrontation. Not only with others, but mostly with me. I confront others because I know it's a necessary part of healing. If I never face my past for what it is, then I won't be dealing with it; hence, I won't be healing from it. Confronting others is not always the best way to get others to see my point of view—this I know. I'm working on it. I do see things in myself. A lot of the time, I don't like what I see in me, so I work on changing it. It's never easy to change. But I'd rather right a wrong than just be wrong and act like I'm right! That's wrong.

10

Visions of Loveliness

I'm having a moment of clarity. In fact, it's a moment of loveliness. I want to have this wonderful niceness and loveliness about me, without losing me. My friend, Kat, has the qualities I lack—loveliness, balance, diplomacy, tact, etc. I don't always wish for them, but they would make me whole. Perhaps that is why Kat is my friend; she balances me. She is all the good, while I am all the learning.

The parts of me that some appreciate are the parts others don't. I know, I know; I can please some of the people all the time, and all of the people some of the time, but never can I please everyone all the time. But what if I don't like the people I'm pleasing some of the time? What if they are the ones where we have too much on one side of the scale? Maybe they are the ones we meet for a reason. We come in and out of people's lives for a reason and then soon leave. Sometimes, the reason is for me to be the bigger person. Or for me to be the teacher. I'm the one who needs the help! Is it possible that others are worse off than me? Is it really possible that I *am* the bigger person? Not always, that's for sure. Sometimes I don't have the capacity to fix the other person, but is that my lesson? Is that what I am supposed to learn? I now know this is true for me. The personality traits I least possess I find in my closest friends I make. Why is learning so very hard? But if it isn't hard, I don't learn. And sometimes I get to learn in the most beautiful ways. From the most beautiful people—the people who bring out the best in me! The people I love most! The ones I choose to have near to me.

11

Just Cry

Often when I'm busy dealing with my life, I have to try hard to avoid crying. But when I just let myself cry, I feel so much better. I release. Once I start, I feel like I won't be able to stop. That is a very scary feeling. I felt that way during my divorce. I kept avoiding my feelings by leaving them at home every night. I couldn't bear them. Until one day, I couldn't avoid them. They came at me full force. I even asked my friend for help. She didn't think I was serious. That made it so much worse. When I finally asked for help, my friend didn't take me seriously. She thought I was kidding. When I started to cry, I couldn't stop for two weeks. I felt like I belonged in an insane asylum or a morgue. It was such an awful feeling to feel I had no control over how I felt. I wanted to jump out of my skin and just run away.

Thankfully, the feeling went away. Then I realized it was part of my healing. I hadn't been feeling my pain at all. I'd been completely avoiding it. I couldn't stay home at night, and I had no other outlet but to go out. Finally, I understood I must feel and deal to heal.

Now, I let myself cry because I know it is important. When I feel it, I let it go. Of course, I cry alone at home. I'm not good at crying in front of people. If I know I need to let it go but can't, I rent a sad movie. That always does the trick.

12

Problems

Today was horrible. For the first time, I went to see Gayle in her new home—a nursing home. As I walked through the halls, it was what I'd expected—a lot of older people. My sister is forty-five; I don't consider her older. Older than me, yes, but not "grandma" old. I tried hard to hold back my tears, but they welled up in my eyes. A guy who asked if he could help me could see I was having a difficult time.

When I found Gayle's room, I stood there and cried for twenty minutes. She was sleeping, and I didn't want to wake her and have her see me crying. I knew that would make her feel bad. Half of her head was shaved, and on the other half, her hair was long. As I stood there and watched her sleep, I thought, *Why? Why this wonderful, sweet, compassionate, lovely woman? What is the lesson to be learned here? Why her? Why God?*

Then the activities director came in and saw me crying. She asked me what had happened to my sister. I told her about the brain tumor from eleven years ago and the clogged shunt. She told me we all have problems. Why does it bother me so much to have people tell me they have problems? I wanted to say, "Shut up! Get away from me!" But I waited to see what her problems are, and as usual, they didn't compare. I just didn't want to hear them. I thought, *Fuck you if you think you have problems!* I use to think I had problems until I really got problems. It makes me so angry when people want to compare their stuff with my stuff. Just don't go there. Let me talk to the lady whose kids were killed by her ex-husband; now that's a problem!

I finally stopped crying, and I tried to wake Gayle by shaking her and saying her name. She muttered something in a groggy voice. Finally, she opened her eyes, but she didn't see me. I told her it was me and I wanted her to open her eyes, but she fell back asleep. I don't know why God is keeping her on this planet. I talked to Karen and told her I don't even know what to pray for anymore. She told me she asked God to take Gayle. I was afraid to say it out loud. That was one of Karen's bravest moments. It's a horrible moment to let your living sister go. But I started thinking it is time to let Gayle go. She has no quality of life. She is in a vegetative state. She can't remember from one moment to the next. And it's so very hard to witness.

13

Thank You

Thank you, God, for giving me the greatest gift humans get to experience. I feel so blessed to have found this man, Jim, whom I love so deeply, who brings out the best in me and loves me back. I realize that some people go a lifetime never feeling like this, some because of fear, others because of their own stupidity or addictions.

Today, Jim left for his three-month trip to Thailand. It was a difficult day, but it was also a wonderful day! I truly felt all the love Jim holds for me in his heart! I can't explain it, but I saw it and felt it in my heart.

There are no words for what I felt today. This time was different. It was so deep. So true. I felt so overwhelmed by his love. I know it doesn't make sense that he leaves for so long, and I often remind him of that in a tongue-in-cheek sort of way. But I believe the saying is true that if you love somebody, set them free, and if they love you, they will come back. Our love went to another level, and it was so lovely! Thank you, God, for giving me this most divine gift of all. And thank you for giving me the experiences I needed to fully understand the magnitude of this treasure I have found. Despite all the crap in my family's life, you have given me light in so many dark moments.

Last night, Jim told me I have the spirituality of the Thai people (the biggest compliment he gives). I explained to him that my friend Julie is my spiritual inspiration. He wants to say thank you to Julie, and so do I. This morning, he looked at me in a way I haven't seen in his eyes before, and the way he said he loved me was more than I could handle. When I left him at the airport gate, he looked back. He never looks back. He's always a mover and a doer in forward motion.

14

Lucky

I have always believed that if you die doing what you love, then you are pretty lucky and are all right when moving on. But what if you don't die that way? What if you die suffering? Is the process different? What if when you die, you just die, and it doesn't matter what you were doing when it happened?

I have always thought someone who died sky diving, riding their motorcycle, or surfing knew the risk but loved doing it. They died living their life the way they knew they should. How they knew, I don't know. They just knew how it felt to feel free. How wonderful! Not everyone gets to experience such a blissful and resolute way of life. In fact, I think most of us miss that sensation altogether. I'm not sure I have really experienced it. But I know I have to ski. I'm not sure if it's because of how I feel when I ski, the beauty of the outdoors in such a vast and amazing setting, or just the fact that I am free.

I understand we don't get to remember our past lives because we are here in this life to learn something new. I know we should not be afraid of death because we have been on the other side before and decided to come back to a human life for a reason. That reason may be to learn something or to help someone else learn something, I'm not sure, but I feel fairly relaxed about all this. Yes, my heart aches. Yes, I get sad. Yes, I am human and far from perfect. But I have felt things I don't hear many people talking about. I have felt my angels. I remember the first time I was pretty certain one was present. Who else would have known just what to say in a moment when I was so lost?

I don't know why this life has so many twists and turns. I'm sure a lot of people feel the same way. All I know is that as hard as life gets, there will be someone to help. Someone to figure things out. Someone to cry with. Someone to pick you up and make you laugh. Someone to love. Someone to help you with your success. Someone to support. Someone to be lazy with or just go to the beach and hang out with. Sometimes it will seem like no one is around. That's when I know I am supposed to be alone to look inside myself. To check in. To get to know myself. To figure out what I am on this earth to learn and maybe even pass on to others to help them go through stuff.

Here is what I have discovered I am not here to do—paint, draw, sing, drop from heights, ski really fast, or perform on stage. However, I believe I am here to face my fears fearlessly, laugh, push people's buttons to make them face a fear or deal with some issue, be free to do what I truly want to do, and to not stop others from what they want.

I am not completely clear on why I am here right now. I get scared. I cry. I don't always know why my lessons seem so harsh. But I don't worry too much. I know one thing for certain…we all have to die… and when we do, it will be okay.

15

Meltdown

This story is a doozy. Jim and I were at our favorite ski resort, having a great time. Perhaps too good of a time. A little wine, few irritations, a little relaxation. A little letting go. That's when the release came about. I went for a walk to get away from all the men in the condo where we were staying. I was the only woman, so I knew I would receive little compassion for what was about to be unleashed. The tears started flowing uncontrollably. I walked up the street to some thigh-deep snow on the roadside. I lay down and had no desire to get up. I felt hopeless. Just hopeless. I didn't feel the need to get up. I fully knew what would happen if I stayed there, but I didn't care. I wasn't suicidal. I was just done. It seemed like every day another family member was getting cancer, needing brain surgery, or having their cancer come back. I thought I was handling it all, but I wasn't. There really isn't a way to handle all that stuff, and crying can just take me down. I thought, *How can I be so willing to give up when my sister is fighting so hard to stay alive?* I was in perfect health. No illness. But I just didn't want to stay alive anymore.

I got up and decided to look for a sign. I was trudging through the snow, it was dark out, and I just wanted to give up. I saw some kind of sign and worked my way over to it. The sign said, "Keep out" so I did. I kept out. I was looking for a sign, and I found it. I turned around, walked back to the condo and put some ice on my face so it wouldn't be swollen from all the crying. I decided it was time to talk to a counselor, and when I got home, I called for help.

I went to a counselor at the Cancer Center. I asked her if she knew any families who have had to endure so much cancer in their immediate family. She said, "No." I asked if it was okay for me to have a meltdown from time to time? She said, "Of course." That's all I can say I took from that experience. I knew it was time to stop counseling again when I felt like I was going in to cheer her up! That desire completely came from me, not her. I wanted to make her smile. I figured her days were all about such sadness and difficulties that didn't make sense that I just wanted to make her life a little easier.

16

Choosing Happiness

Happiness is a choice. Until you choose it, it will be hard to come by. I often wonder how to tell new friends about all the cancer that exists in my immediate family. I find myself just blurting out that one sister has had leukemia, colon cancer, uterine cancer, and now cancer again in her pelvic region. I guess that means when they take out all your organs in that area, the only thing left to call it is the "pelvic region." Then there's my eldest sister, who is a complete vegetable because she had a brain tumor. Did I mention my mom, who also had a brain tumor, and now she can't speak—the one thing she really enjoyed doing, especially in the morning. Oh yeah, and my dad is being treated for his bladder cancer right now. People don't have a clue unless I tell them.

And now I'm feeling sad and hopeless. All the lessons I have learned have gone down the drain for six months. I'm miserable, depressed, sad, and hopeless. My will to live has become weak. Go ahead—give me the cancer! I won't fight it! That attitude is why I know I won't be getting it. I won't fight it. It's not my calling in life. Karen's the fighter, not me.

I felt done with this life, but then it hit me. I heard someone say, "Happiness is a choice!" I've been pondering those words for a month now, and they are really hitting home.

When we are young, we dream about what we might be when we grow up. We have expectations of ourselves and others. We think about who we may end up marrying, the children we could have, and the career we might choose. Sometimes when we get there, it's not at all what we thought it would be. The trials and tribulations, the fears, the issues, the letdowns, sadness, sickness, and ultimately death. How we handle them determines our mental, emotional, and physical well-being. Choosing to be positive and not let things take you down is very hard, but it is so important. And, yes, it is a choice!

It's a choice. It's a *choice*! *It's a choice!* It is truly a choice to be happy! That's the choice I've been making since 1990. I have a great zest for life. Karen and I both do. Despite all she's been through, she still finds joy in life. I've been following her, making sure I laugh a lot and find the humor in little things.

But one day recently, I lost that ability. I couldn't find things funny anymore. It was too much. I couldn't handle more bad stuff. I lost my will to survive it all. When my counselor asked what I was feeling, the only word that came to mind was hopeless. I'm not very good at feeling things, but I felt hopeless. My family is falling apart, and they all seem to be dying at once. Somehow, that doesn't seem fair. Not at such a young age for some of them. Why can't it be spread around a little? Sorry, but I don't know how much more I can take without sharing all this. I keep going back to the sayings, "God doesn't give you more than you can handle" and "I am where I'm supposed to be." I truly believe each of those is true. God doesn't give me more than I can handle. Apparently, I can handle a lot! Go ahead, what else ya got? Just kidding! I've had enough. I hope.

Hey, at least I have hope back! Anyway, I'm working on choosing to be happy again. I have discovered that it's way worse to have all this cancer crap in my life and to feel miserable. I also know that it's much better to choose to be happy and just learn to deal with it all. I have a sneaking suspicion that I'm meant to do something really wonderful on this earth. I'm not sure what it is, but I have a strong sense it's something really good. Maybe it's writing this book? I only hope I can help someone going through something by writing it.

17

Mother's Day

I just wrote a note to my mom in her Mother's Day card. I found it so hard to do. I feel so sad for her now. I want to tell her that her illness sucks and being unable to speak after her brain surgery all sucks. However, I know it will only make her sad that I am sad, so I put on my happy face and try to cheer up a sad situation.

I wish I could tell her how much I want to hear her talk in the mornings, though I wasn't quite ready to listen back then. She was the morning person. I was not. Even though she is still alive, I feel like some things are too late now. When my friends tell me they are going to lunch or out shopping with their moms, I feel that opportunity is gone for me. I don't think she got to enjoy her life to the fullest. There are things left undone, and unless God sends a miracle, I don't think she will ever go to Rome to see the Pope, or take a riverboat ride down the Mississippi. I have learned if there is a place I want to see, I should go now. There is no tomorrow, only today.

I feel so bad for her when she is trying to tell me something and I have to play a guessing game with her. I can see the utter frustration in her eyes. Then I just want to cry and hold her and tell her how sorry I am. Even though I don't believe in living life with regrets, I'm having a hard time dealing with this. I know it's too late to go back. I can only live without regret from this moment on. There's really no point in going back in time, except to learn. I go home every month to make sure I don't put off visiting my mom. None of us know how much time we get on this earth, so what we do with our time is so important. I spend time with my family as often as I can to avoid any regrets later. Even though it's so hard to see my mom and my sister Gayle, who is in a nursing home, I know it's not all about me and my feelings. I come home to escape my family's cancers. I can only handle so much before it starts to take me down. I go on with my life because I have to, and I must remember to enjoy the little things.

Someone once told me I have a zest for life! I believe in living each and every day to the fullest by enjoying each and every moment I get. When I'm with my friends, I'm in the moment and I laugh as much as possible. I am not hiding or avoiding my feelings; I am just living. Lately, I've been very peaceful and have been wondering if I have been avoiding myself. Then I realized I am okay. I am going to be okay. Even though I don't think any of my family will ever truly recover from their cancer, I have this horrible feeling that when they start to die, they will all go close together. I don't know if that will be a relief or tremendous, heartfelt, gut-wrenching pain. Then I will have to find a new family. I will miss them so very much, but it will mean closing a chapter in my life. And that will be a relief.

18

Changing Your Ways

When I was growing up, my dad wasn't always the kind of dad I wanted. In fact, I suspect he might be the reason I don't want children of my own. He never made having kids look easy. I was never under any impression that his kids were a joy to him. We were more of a burden. He would step up to the plate when he felt like it, but fatherhood never came naturally to him. To this day, I'm okay with that. I truly believe I am who I am supposed to be. Without him, I never would have become the person I am. True, parts of me would have been nicer, less argumentative, less aggressive, and less self-righteous. But I also wouldn't have so much to work on, and that would be boring. I like a challenge. I love personal growth!

Something very interesting has occurred with my dad since my mom got her brain tumor. It wasn't enough for her to have a brain tumor; no, she had to have not one, but two brain surgeries. Even then, it wasn't the breaking point. A blood clot that made my mom mostly disabled and unable to speak caused my dad finally to step up to the plate. Then he started to be the man of the house. Now he takes care of the household chores the best he can. He takes care of my mom the best he can. For him, it is an amazing feat. I am truly amazed by the man he has finally become.

I should point out here how much of a tyrant he used to be. He yelled at my poor mom every single day. He would call her every name in the book and sit on his ass expecting her to wait on him like he was a king.

"Gerrie, get me this or get me that! What the bleep did you do with this? Where the bleep did you put that?" Even as a child, I understood this was not normal behavior. I wonder how I didn't turn out to be more of an asshole than I am.

But now I am finding inspiration in this aging man. If he can change at his age, anyone can. Never think you are too young or too old to change. You will amaze yourself if you just try.

19

The Connection

The moment I met Jim, it was "love at first sight." My immediate reaction was "Wow! He's cute," and from that moment on, I was gaga in love! He was almost everything I wanted in a man, and the things he lacked I didn't find too important. The night we met, the whole world could have stopped and I never would have known. I was so into him. I didn't even know there was life outside of what we had at that moment. The second time we were together, we kissed. I truly felt like the room was turning around us, just like in the movies. Since I had never felt that, I didn't think it really existed. But I found out it was true.

As time passed, I discovered he brought out the best in me—something I didn't know existed. I wasn't always delightful, but he made me want to be a better person. I don't know how it worked, but it was true for me. It wasn't that I was trying to impress him; I wasn't even aware of it for a long time.

I didn't really believe in the wholehearted, unconditional, sickening, want-to-die love thing. I didn't buy it. I had already been married and divorced and learned there are no guarantees in life. But now I learned there was love at first sight! Six years later, I still love my man so very much! But that love is not always the way I thought it would be.

Six weeks into our relationship, he left for Thailand for six weeks. *Okay,* I thought. *I can get through this.* It was so hard, though. I thought about him every waking moment. I must have driven my friends crazy just talking about him. I felt nauseous just thinking about him. Like I said, I was gaga.

A year later, he went to Thailand for two months. *Okay,* I thought, *I can get through this too. I love him so very much!* Once again, I was sickened over the experience of being left by the man I felt so in love with. I truly think it was something I was meant to go through. How else could I possibly feel so strongly about another human and intentionally be put through this kind of torture? Besides, I couldn't afford to go and he didn't offer to pay. Although I don't think I would be comfortable accepting the gesture if he did offer because I wasn't raised that way. Oh, and he never really invited me; he said, "*You can go*," if I asked. That did not feel like an invitation and was a little hurtful.

The next year, he let me know he was going for three months. Yeah, me too—speechless. I couldn't figure out how you could love someone the way I loved him and leave them on purpose. Once again, I looked for what I was to learn. I learned how much I truly love this man although I'm not sure why. I never doubted it until I this very moment as I write it down. I am finding it hard to breathe right now. I'm not sure how to feel. I guess he always reassured me along the way. I also learned to trust my gut. I knew how it felt to be cheated on, and I never felt that way with Jim. I trusted him. Maybe it's not a matter of trust. Maybe it was immature of me. I wondered if he could love someone as much as he loved himself. Did he love himself? His mom kind of messed him up. At Christmas, I watched for similarities between him and his mom and saw many. His mom taught him to love to travel. She also taught him the need to be free. There were other smaller similarities I found interesting.

My point is no matter how in love you might feel in the beginning, there will always be personality challenges. Stay in a relationship for a long time before you decide to marry. I still love Jim to the utmost, but I feel left out of certain parts of his life. And even though he tries to share them with me, they remain a wall of uncertainty. Any wall will be a challenge.

20

Keeping It Real

What makes people fall in love—a glance, a touch, a kiss, chemistry? I'm still not sure. But I lean toward chemistry, and everything after that falls into place. It's easy to stay in love for the first year. Everyone is on their best behavior. We all are being the best we can be. We are doing the "dance" to keep the one we attracted interested and perhaps to marry them. Then what? We get married. Then what? Do we have to stay on our best behavior forever? I wish. This is when it falls apart for some. It all depends on how much of ourselves we were keeping to ourselves. If we would just let the other know what they are getting into while we are dating, the divorce rate might not be so high.

If we let our bad habits show through in the relationship right away, how might things play out? If we let our insecurities out in the first month, how long would that love interest stay? Not long? Then why not wait until you meet the next "love of your life" to teach you to stay on your best behavior until you are with the person you should be with, instead of falsely advertising yourself as someone you are not. I have had to learn this lesson the hard way, but it is most important to learn it. Otherwise, you can become unlovable. If we don't learn our lessons when we are young, it gets harder and harder to learn them as we age.

So, how do we stay in love? Keep it fresh. Stay healthy. Don't let yourself go. If something is bothering you, don't wait until it builds up and then you explode and say things you feel bad about. The other person won't understand that. Maybe they will the first, second, or third time, but after that, you're on your own. Don't withhold sex. If something bothers you, find an effective and healthy way to communicate it. Always show love and affection! Kiss, hug, and touch! Keep it real. Don't you want someone to treat you that way?

21

Feeling Down

It caught up to me again. I was going along just fine, working and having fun. But I feel I can't stop weeping. Part of me is depressed, and I want to fight it with all my might! I know what happens when I get this way. I have no control over myself. I can't pull myself out of this place, no matter how hard I try. My mom is back in the hospital, after two more seizures the other morning. I didn't know I was feeling this way until my friend came by and I snapped at her. Good thing she's not the type of girl who takes my kind of crap.

So, I immediately took a look at myself to discover what my problem was. It wasn't too difficult to find. I went to bed weeping and woke up crying—not a good mix. I'm pretty sick of this. Last week, I cried a lot because we had to put down Jim's dog, April. Then I thought I would have to put my dog, Rufus, to sleep, but she recovered. I couldn't leave her with my dad in the condition she was in; she couldn't walk, and my dad has enough to deal with because of my mom's problems. So, I thought I had gotten the crying out and would be okay, but I was wrong. I seem to have opened the floodgates in my eyes. In addition, there's no one to support me right now. My friends all have their own stuff going on and can't be there for me, except for Kate; she called me last night to make sure I was okay. That made me cry some more.

Plus, Jim has been gone for ten weeks and won't be back for another three. He's the one I'm really missing. But he doesn't want to hear about the bad stuff. He's on vacation and doesn't deal well with all this stuff. What man does? I did have an amazing kiss with him in my dream last night. I am looking forward to the real thing when he returns. I'll close with that thought. I'm looking forward to an amazing kiss with Jim, and I can't wait! Three weeks from today....

22

Angels

I can't quite seem to figure out when is the correct or best or most appropriate time to cry, or even when I have time to cry. And whom do I cry for first? For my sister Karen? I have to stay strong for her. The first sign of weakness and we will all crumble. For myself? If I'm crying, who will take care of us all? I feel so distraught right now.

I was already struggling before my sister came to live with me. She just started her first round of chemo yesterday. And what a day that was! Thank God the chemo went well. Karen was scared, and I don't blame her. The last time she had chemo, it made her toxic and almost killed her. We got out of The City of Hope surprisingly all right. We went to find a pharmacy open at night, and while we were looking, her ileostomy bag broke—all over her lap. That stuff is pretty gnarly and burns the skin, so we headed back to The City of Hope. They took her in and cleaned her up.

Meanwhile, I wanted to take care of her prescriptions for nausea. She's likely to get nauseous from chemo. A kind nurse told me about a pharmacy that's open late, so I called to make sure they had her stuff. They did. So I went. I was in the store for a while, waiting, shopping, and reading. When I turned to leave, three adults climbed over the pharmacy counter and ran into the back! I couldn't figure out what I was seeing. I thought they were stealing something. Then someone told me the store was being robbed! Needless to say, I didn't know what to do! So, I followed the other people and climbed over the counter.

Within ten seconds, all the pharmacy personnel were gone and the robbery was over! It freaked me out! I was shaking! I had never been that close to an armed robbery before. The police came and questioned everyone, and then I left.

It took a while to get back to Karen, and when I did, she wondered where I had been. She didn't have cell phone reception in the hospital so I couldn't call to tell her. By then, she was cleaned up and ready to go. We finally got on the road at 11 p.m. I kept thinking my angels had been working overtime to keep us from leaving when we tried. First, the wound care nurse never showed up. Then, the ileostomy bag broke. Then the nurse told me which pharmacy to go to, and finally, the robbery. All events keeping us off the road until 11 p.m. I figured there was a very good reason for this, and the angels have much bigger plans for us. It makes life a lot easier when I take it in stride and just know my angels are looking out for me.

23

Losing Rufus

I'll never forget the day I met Rufus. She was in a cage in a pet adoption place, and when I saw her, I knew she was the dog I went there for. I knew her before I even got there. When I took her out of the cage, she dragged me down the street, but I didn't judge her character from that behavior. I figured I'd be running too to get out of that cage! They told me she had been abused, and she had been in that cage for over a month.

I took her home and loved her from then on. I used to say I gave birth to her. I truly felt she came from my womb. Our connection ran as deep as a connection can. She was somewhat unruly and a free spirit, but I understood her, and I always figured out how to avoid problems with her. When she would escape from the yard, I put in an electric fence. When she tried to dominate other dogs, which caused fights, I kept her away from them. The exception was her best friend, Shady. He was a Great Dane, and they loved each other so much that they would roll around and play for hours.

I was only twenty-four when I found Rufus. She was there when I got married. She was the reason I stayed in my marriage two-and-a-half years longer than I wanted to—I knew how hard it would be to rent with a pet in my town. So, I stayed for her sake. When I finally left, I had to leave her there, but I would go visit her all the time and just cry. All she wanted to do was play! The day I brought her over to my new home, I went to put her in the car, but she thought I was putting her back in my ex-husband's yard, so she sat down, pulled back, and wouldn't go. I knew taking her home with me was the best thing I could ever do. She just wanted to be with me. I didn't have a yard, and I wasn't allowed to have a pet, but I was going to make it work, and I did.

At that time, I had just brought my business home, so I knew I could walk her three times a day. The Universe was taking care of me. It all fell into place. For more than five years, I walked her every day—morning, noon, and night. In the beginning, she wanted to go forever, but Mommy had to get work done. We figured out a way to make it work for both of us. She was a morning girl, but I was not. If I couldn't walk her, I would find someone who could. We made it work.

The last year of her life, Rufus started to show signs of aging and slowed down tremendously. I just hoped God would make it clear to me when it was time to put her down. That day came today. Because of our amazing connection and all the love in my heart, I knew to prepare myself for this day. Now I know there is no preparing for this day. I thought it might even be a relief because she had not been herself for so long. I couldn't have been more wrong. I feel like I have lost my best friend. I never felt alone when she was here. Even when she became deaf, I still felt comforted by her presence. She was very protective of me, sometimes to a fault.

My heart is aching, and I feel so very sad. The pain I am feeling is unbearable. Unimaginable. I can't stop crying. For two days, I stayed by her side, cried, and told her everything I wanted to say to her before she went. She was put to sleep at the foot of my bed, where she slept every night with me. I was holding her head to comfort her, saying goodbye, and telling her I love her. She went very peacefully. She is out of her pain and discomfort, but I miss her so, so much. I never felt this kind of pain before, but I hope she is up in heaven playing with her best dog friend, Shady, and having the time of her new life. And maybe at night when she is tired, she will come sleep at the foot of my bed and keep me company. We went through a lot—the good, the bad, the happy, and the sad—and she always stayed by my side. I miss you, Rufus. I will always miss you with all my heart and soul....

Usually writing makes me feel better because I get my feelings out and onto paper, but not this time. I still hurt so much. Last night, I woke at 3 a.m. and heard an owl—perhaps the same owl I heard when my brother-in-law Jim passed. I knew then I would be all right; it will just take some time. Rufus was part of my life for fourteen years. I can't imagine these feelings of loss will go away too soon. But I know life will go on. I just need to take time to mourn her and honor the wonderful time we had together.

24

Health

Our health is all we truly have. So many people are willing to eat poorly and not make any necessary changes to improve their health. Things like fake sugars, fast foods, and partially hydrogenated oils are chemicals that will eventually cause disease in our bodies if we don't stop ingesting them. It makes me crazy when someone says, "I'm too set in my ways to change what I eat." It's stupidity to think you are invincible. The other saying I hate is "I'm going to die from something anyway." Yeah, I will die too somehow, but while I'm here, I don't want to live like a vegetable. My mom can't speak, my sister can hardly think, and my other sister is so uncomfortable all the time that it wholly consumes her. She can't live a normal life. Her everyday wish is to live without feeling horrible.

Unfortunately, some people will find out the hard way that they should have made a few changes along the way. I can always learn from others' mistakes. I don't need to make the same choices and have the same outcome. I learned from my siblings to go to college. I have friends who are smarter than me and have helped guide me. I've learned moderation is the key to life.

Still, I will be sad when some of my friends get sick because they were too stubborn to listen to healthy advice. I know not everyone wants my advice; in fact, the only people who listen are the ones who already get that health is a choice. And you can change your way of eating. Don't wait until it's too late. Start making healthy choices now so your loved ones don't have to watch you become sick. Lead by example for your children. Find out about healthy living. Eat organic. Then, at least you will know you did everything you could to live a healthy life.

25

Living Life Fully

What is love? Is it a distraction from the pain we feel in this life? I ask because I am unsure at this point. My and Jim's love has become boring and complacent. I am so scared to even type these words. I'm not convinced I'm the bored one. I see my love unreciprocated on all levels.

Karen is fighting for her life right now. She is going to have major surgery to get the tumor out. They will have to remove her bladder, her rectum, and a tumor the size of a Nerf football, as described by her surgeon. Her hope was to reconnect her body to make it work again without bags. Regardless, she has been in the best mood even after such a difficult week for both of us. We didn't get along and even fought. It is really hard for me to be such a bitch to her. I know this could be the end of her life. It is such a huge learning experience for me to keep my mouth shut. I even had a woman I hardly know tell me to think before I speak. I know to do that better than anyone. Sometimes I don't think.

But I am thinking now. Perhaps I have done all I can do in my current relationship. Perhaps it is time to move on. It is so difficult to consider leaving when there is nothing wrong. Although, Jim does leave me every summer for months to have fun in another country. But I fully appreciate that he is living his life. Maybe I should live mine.

26

Be True

Wow. I've been in the most amazing relationship for the last seven years. Jim has brought out the best in me and that's not an easy task! I was so gaga in love in the beginning. He was everything I ever dreamed of in a man. I am crying as I write this. But it's not sadness; it's almost freeing. I've known for a year or more that this relationship cannot survive on my love alone. Now don't get me wrong. He loves me so much, but he loves his freedom more. I'm okay with that. I've learned so much from my loving experience, and I will never be the same.

We have no real reason to part ways except that he leaves every summer to go have fun. I have always believed it is to rejuvenate his soul. I know what you may be thinking because I have had to deal with people and their opinions of what he does over there. The things people have said are not nice. Believe me, I have heard it all, from "Do you know how beautiful the hookers are in Thailand?" to "I know what he's really doing over there" (wink wink). I got so sick of hearing it that I just stopped telling people about his journey. I know from the past how it feels to be cheated on, and I have learned to listen to my gut. My gut says he's over there surfing, playing beach volleyball, and kite surfing.

When people say such things, I think, *Don't you know that you are talking about the man I love with all my heart and soul?* Even his mother asked me how it makes me feel to have him leave every summer. I told her I'm okay with it, and when the time comes that I'm not, then I will have to leave the relationship.

Well, it's taken me seven years to get to the point where I'm not okay with it. I will be frank. I feel like his life in Thailand means a hell of a lot more to him than our relationship. Yes, it is so hurtful, but I loved so deeply that I couldn't move on. It never felt good for him to leave. But I had two choices: I could stay, or I could leave. I am *not* here to change anyone, and I take great pride in that fact. I know when he leaves, he is rejuvenating himself and living *his* life. I completely admire that! If I could live my life that way, I would!

Yes, the question "Why don't you go?" has come up—a million times! First, I couldn't afford to go. Then I'm asked, "Why doesn't he pay for you to go?" I couldn't let someone pay my way; that's just who I am. The other problem came when he really didn't want me to go. He always said, "You can come," but I never felt welcomed. I figured it was because he didn't want his life there disturbed with having to entertain a girlfriend.

I hope it wasn't that. He might miss me; I don't know. He shuts down at the first sign of deep conversation or conflict. I've never wanted to argue with him. In fact, in seven years, we have only had one real argument.

Now I am at the point where I need to be true to myself. I cannot think about this decision and not cry. It is the most agonizing decision I have ever had to make. How can I leave the man I truly love? My only question is, "Does he love me as much?" On the surface, it doesn't seem like he feels the same as I do. But I was there every single day of our relationship. And I know how he loves me. I think I just had another revelation: It is the only way he knows how to love. Deep down, I knew that and thought I could overlook it. Or maybe I thought it was enough? Or maybe we just got complacent? Did he get bored, or did I?

Another problem is my sister just had an intense, ten-hour surgery in which her bladder, rectum, and a "huge" tumor were removed. My fear that she would not survive the surgery was very real. Deep down, I felt if she didn't make it, Jim would not come back to support me. Not based on our entire relationship. This was a hard cold fact for me to realize—and not like. It broke me. It might be the very reason I am at this place in our relationship. No, I never asked him if he would come back under those circumstances; I felt I would just be setting myself up for disappointment like I have never known.

Wow. I think I am finally admitting I have been so disappointed in this relationship. I know this man has his issues. Who doesn't? I certainly do. But what can I do? I have been so in love for so long. I am sobbing so deeply right now. It's been a long time since I have really let myself just feel how much this truly hurts me. My friend told me today she thinks I deserve a good guy. I thought, *I have a good guy! He sparkles! He is a treasure! I love him so much it hurts*. Maybe it's not such a good hurt. Maybe you shouldn't love someone so much it actually hurts. Maybe that's not such a good thing. I thought it was a "good" hurt.

How many times have we heard that love hurts?

All I know is I love this man, but his long summers away have put too much distance between us. And just when I thought I had found the love of my life, it seems I'm back in the saddle. This is why I will never get married again. If he had asked, I would have said yes! Even right now. If he were to call and say, "I'm over this thing I do every summer. I'm coming home, and I want to marry you!" I would say yes. How sad is that? But I know I'm not alone. Love is truly the most wonderful and amazing feeling we get to experience on this earth! And I will keep on loving. Even if it takes the rest of my life.

PART II

LEARNING FROM LIFE'S CRAP

27

Sunset One

I just spent the last six days at The City of Hope with Karen. She had surgery to put in a poop bag so she can eat again. She now has a new understanding of starvation so she wants to help people who are starving. The surgeons told us the surgery went fine. Her recovery has been a little slow. She's still on ice chips after three days. She was hoping to be eating something with substance by today, but she's not quite there. She seems high as a kite from the drugs they are giving her, but they are weaning her off of them each day. Yesterday and today, they got her out of bed and onto a chair. She sat for thirty minutes today and was so exhausted that she passed out and snored for the next few hours. We take turns spending the night with her because it's a long night in the hospital. They wake her every hour, which wakes you up. Then, if she needs ice chips, you just get up to help her. You do whatever she needs you to do. My biggest fear is that each request could be her last, so I do anything she asks of me. And I'm happy to do it all. Underneath all the drugs, I can still see my kooky sister. She is still there.

Today, I had to go home to pay rent and bills and take care of any business that might have come in while I've been gone. While I was driving home, I came upon the most beautiful magic hour I've ever seen. It actually brought me to tears it was so amazing. I've never seen the ocean so dark blue, and the sky was so orange after the sun went down. I was in complete and utter awe of it. I was afraid I would rear-end someone while watching it as I drove down the coast. I realized it was God talking to me, letting me know He is still there. At least that's how I want to see it. He and all my angels were there to make sure I was able to see it. I left Los Angeles at 4:10 p.m. on a Friday and hit absolutely no traffic! That's unheard of! And I've lived in a beach city all thirty-nine years of my life and have never seen a sunset like that one. It's not often a sunset brings me to tears. I also realized I have not been completely tarnished. I will go on to live my life to its fullest. Maybe even more so than if all this shit hadn't happened to my family. Perhaps, that is the lesson to be learned. Life is so fragile.

28

Self-Destruction

I finally hit my wall. I've been going to see my sister every weekend for two months and just can't do it anymore. I didn't know this meltdown was coming, but it came. When my friend took me to a concert this weekend, I cried through the whole show. I pretty much cried through the entire weekend. I was having fun skateboarding, and I didn't care if I hurt myself. In fact, I think I wanted to hurt myself. I just didn't care anymore. I can't care anymore. I've been avoiding feeling all there is to feel since Karen went into surgery, and I can't seem to ignore it anymore. I feel like I am punishing myself. I went for a soft sand run, and it was my intention to punish myself. I figured if I didn't have anything left physically, I couldn't break down any more emotionally.

I don't want to feel like this anymore. I just want to go away right now and never look back. I'm so tired of this life. I didn't choose this, and

I wouldn't wish it on anyone. It really sucks right now. I'm not sure how I'm even going to function today. I usually like to distract myself from life through work or fun. But I don't know if that will even work. I do know I have an amazing ability to live in the moment! When I am somewhere, I am there! I don't think about everything else going on in my life. I am fully absorbed in the moment and that's it! I love this about myself, and I have to figure out how to get back there. I've been in this place before, so I know it will go away. I just hope it doesn't last too long. I really don't like it here, but tomorrow will be a new day, and it has to get better than this....

29

The Fight

I am in such an interesting place in my life right now. I'm not sure I can even describe it, but I will try. It's so confusing, yet so clear. Upsetting, yet so calm. Changing, yet so much the same. Sad, but I'm okay with the process. I'm in the middle of not talking to Karen, thinking about moving on from my seven-year relationship, and figuring out how to take back my life.

I just spent the last three months driving down every weekend to be with Karen, after her surgery. Right about the time she was being released from the hospital, it became my wedding season. I photograph weddings for a living. On those days, my life doesn't get to matter; it's all about the happy couple. I just spent three months of weekends doing that. I don't have any problem giving myself to my loved ones, or anyone else who needs me. I actually enjoy giving. It feels good to me. But I also have to work to earn a living.

Karen and I haven't spoken for a month now. We used to talk every single day, usually two to four times a day. Since I had to go to work, she got upset and apparently doesn't think my life is worth living. My work or paying my bills doesn't seem to matter to her. The only thing that matters for her is fighting for her life. I agree. But we all have to fight for our lives at some point. For some, it might be some shitty disease. And I will be there with her when I can. I need to be appreciated for that, not given this guilt-tripping behavior.

But I don't take it personally. I know she is going through the thickest stuff in her life. It's the darkest, most cave-like dwelling place anyone can go. This I know. I know because I see and watch. I know because I never want to go there. And I never will. I just won't. Perhaps my sheer will can keep me out of that place. I choose never to go there. I've seen too much on the inside of the hospital. It is not a pleasant place to go. Not even to work. I could never do the jobs of the people who work there. I completely understand how they can do it; it's just not for me. It would take me down. Perhaps because I've spent too much time there with my loved ones.

I haven't balanced my checkbook for four months. I've paid bills with the wrong amount of money. And I just don't care. I could ask to have the late fees removed…blah blah blah...but I really don't care. I might care someday. Just not today. Right now, I want to leave and never come back. I don't care about living, and I'm sure it's understandable why I might feel that way. But I know this, too, will pass. And I can't wait until it does. I am truly looking forward to it. I know my angels are here for a reason. They are looking out for me. They will guide me through this experience and get me out of my holes that I land in. So will my friends. I think that's why I surround myself with so many friends. They are my family—my chosen family.

30

The Weight of My Sister

I went out tonight thinking I could leave my stuff behind and go have some fun. Apparently, that wasn't possible. I had enough wine to realize the weight of my sister's stuff was just too much to bear. It became apparent I needed someone to help me hold up her stuff that was being put on me. Our parents were no longer available. My dad is taking care of our mom, which is more than he can handle. That is so sad in itself. Our oldest sister, who would normally take on this stuff, is an invalid. I tried so hard to take it on myself, only to find I can't. I really need someone—lots of someones—to help me. I cannot do that by myself. I need every single one of my friends to hold me up because I don't know how long I can hold up myself. It is a lot to take on. I am at my breaking point and don't quite know how to hold myself together anymore. Please help. Any friend willing to step up and help hold me up while I hold up my sister is sincerely called upon at this time. All I need is a hand to hold.

31

Favors

Don't do her any favors by staying in a relationship with her. Just so you know, it's not really doing her any favors at all. You are keeping her from the rest of her life. Moving on is all she has. The rest of her life is all she has!

I know I don't want a great relationship to end, but if you aren't really in it anymore, then it's not a great relationship anymore. Move on! That way, she, too, can move on. Yes, it's gonna be hard for you to see her cry. And yes, it's going to hurt her. And yes, it's going to be very difficult to say. And, yes, it's going to be very sad. But it is how you feel. And it is your life too! So be a human and an adult and say the words—whether she is ready to hear them or not, whether you are ready to say them or not. Just let her go. Don't cheat on her. Don't say you love her when she asks. Don't try to make her believe how much you love her when she persists. She already knows. Deep down inside, she knows. That's why she is asking. She is opening the door. She has a deep undesired need to know. She can't help herself. Even though the answer you have is not the one she wants to hear, she knows. And the longer you string her along with the empty answers of how much you love her, the longer you keep her from the rest of her life.

On the other hand, she may not be ready to hear you are done and ready to move on. So, she may not let you say what you need to say until she has processed your disabling words. And then she will let you move out of her life—even as you say she is your best friend and you love her now more than ever. And then she asks, "Are we really doing this?" "Why are we doing this again?" You need to stay strong and do what is right. Answer honestly and from your heart. Even if that means letting her go, letting her move on. We only have a certain amount of time on this planet. We only get to experience a limited amount of life. If we keep on keeping others for our own delight, then we might just be keeping others from living life.

32

Gut-Wrenching

Life is so strange. First, you think you have one thing. Then, life turns in another direction. Then, it ends up being something totally different. Right now, I'm finding this to be true by going in so many directions.

It's so confusing when you follow your gut. And, oh, so scary. But your gut is everything. This I know. I don't even question it. I just know how difficult it is to know my gut. I want one thing. I need another. Then what I thought was true turns out to be something else altogether. How can I ever know which road to take? I love someone, so I marry them, but it turns out so wrong, and I have to leave them. Then I find the person I thought I am meant to be with, and it becomes foggy again. I stay in a long-term relationship without the marriage because it scares the hell out of me, and then I'm back to wondering if I'm with the right person. Then I find I have psychic moments, and I think I'm okay with my thoughts. But then I'm back to wondering. The responses are not what I expect, so I wonder again.

I know I'm not alone. I know there are others just like me. And the times are so hard—gut-wrenching. But wait. Clear my mind. Get clear with myself and figure out what it really is that makes me happy. Still sad and confused, but that's okay. It will be better tomorrow. Sleep has an amazing effect on thoughts. Become thoughtful. Think! This is my life. What is it I want for me? Happiness? Sadness? I know happiness is so much better, and I will strive for it every single day! If this is how you feel, you're not alone. Remember to tell yourself, "It's okay!"

33

Damage Control

I just read my journals from when Jim and I started dating and became serious. Everything I felt and saw back then came true. I had forgotten about that stuff since it was seven years ago. I was just shocked to read it again. Now I know I was supposed to go through those feelings and emotions to pull me through to this very moment. I cannot explain it any other way.

Was I there to be a playmate and friend to Jim? Was the experience to help me become a much better person? Wow. I just got it. I am a much better person now because of that relationship. Yes, I am sobbing.... I loved so very deeply. I set my heart free with him. But as I look back, I see I called it. I saw it from seven years away. He was never able to be in a long-term relationship because of the damage his mom did to him in his childhood. That didn't bother me. I guess I thought that would be fine since I never needed to get married again. I learned from that experience. My stomach tightens just thinking about what he must have gone through.

Life affects us in adverse ways, especially in our childhood. Looking into your childhood can set you free as an adult. Yes, it's painful and it hurts like hell, but not as much as the second time around. You will still be an adult, and your life will go forward if you let it. Don't let your past control your life…adversely.

34

Sweet Love

As I watch and photograph young couples getting married and in that place of sweet love, I can't help but wonder if this love is "the love" that will last them the rest of their lives. It is wonderful to watch and hope they have found that one love. I really do believe we get our loves of our lives, but I also believe we get more than one. I feel fairly certain we have loves in our friendships, our family, our hearts, when we "just know" we know that person we have just met.

I am single again, but I feel I am in a good place. I get to do what I want and not feel bad about doing it. Maybe that's a sign I was not in the right relationship. That I'm single again is a sure sign it wasn't meant to be. I wonder what it is. What is that magical element that holds people together? Is it the understanding that no matter what happens, they will stay together? Is it that the love never fades? So far, those are the only two things I can come up with to understand what makes love last. Even though I feel like I am in a good place right now, I will want love in my heart again. When my heart heals again, I know I will want and will be ready for that magical thing called love.... After all, it is the greatest thing we get to experience while we are alive on this planet. So, if you haven't had it yet, you better go find it, before life passes you by.

35

Love

I have been photographing weddings for fifteen years now, and I've learned a few things along the way. Some people are simply beautiful together. Despite all the flaws, they find the most wonderful qualities in each other. I know as well as the next lovesick couple that relationships are not always meant to last forever, but so many of my past clients have stayed together. Hell, I've been married, divorced, gaga, and now not so gaga, and lots of things in between, but I still find love so wonderfully attractive and beautiful! I am still in awe of the amazing feelings it brings out. We have almost no control over it. The emotions and tribal lust that come from it are unreal. That's it—unreal! There is no way we humans ever manifested this love energy ourselves; it had to come from somewhere else. I mean, our feelings completely take over. I find it unbelievable.

I sit here overwhelmed with emotion for my friend Kat, who has just gone through the most incredible moments of her life. She had to leave a miserable marriage this year. It was so bad I almost lost my friend of twenty years. I didn't know if our friendship would recover because I didn't "recognize" her anymore.

But this summer, we had the most amazing time! I'd like to say I helped her through her divorce. But I know we got each other through some pretty shitty stuff. Karen's surgery was this summer, and I needed to have some F-U-N! I found it was the only way to balance out my life. I started working in a friend's office and going to see my sister every weekend from June to August, so I knew I needed to do something for myself. Yes, the fun included partying, and I needed to do some numbing. So, I did. Work during the week. Drive down on the weekend. Do my workout on the beach, which is so healing for me. Go hang out with my sister, and then go have some fun with Kat! I cannot tell you how much I needed something to look forward to, other than sitting in the hospital for hours at a time, week after week. That can make one go crazy. I was about to go crazy. I started going through an angry stage, but I recognized it in time, so it didn't last long. Thank God. I knew my angels were with me, so I didn't worry too much. I know they take care of me. I knew they would help me get through this.

Having gone through a divorce, I understood Kat needed to feel good about herself again. She needed to feel desired and attractive. A bad marriage can take away your self-esteem and desires—the very desires that make us feel alive. I know some psychologists out there will have a name for this, but I'm pretty sure we humans are pretty simple. And, yes, I'm sure I could use some counseling right now. So, I needed something to look forward to, and Kat needed to get back on the market. To make a long story short, Kat met Spartacus (not his real name). They connected instantly! All the cliches...fireworks...love or lust at first sight...blah, blah, blah. They were gaga. It was gross. But it was lovely to see. Normally, I would tell them to quit the public display, but it was such an amazing display to see. I could even feel it. I still can't explain that one. After all, I'm well out of gaga now. I just kept telling Kat to enjoy the moment. But I was a little concerned because it turned out Spartacus had a girlfriend he was more buddies with than in love with. Still, I know men rarely leave.

That's why I couldn't believe what happened. On Kat's birthday, we had a great celebration! A band was playing, and everyone was having a great time. Kat knew Spartacus had to get ready for a trip he was going on with his girlfriend, so she had to let him go. And she did, with a little advice from her friend. The party wore on and moved to other locations.... Next thing I knew, I found Kat outside talking on the phone. When I asked, "Who are you talking to?" Her answer made me feel like I was in my favorite movie, *Sixteen Candles*. She said, "Spartacus just left his relationship. He's coming back here. He's done." I was completely floored. I started welling up with tears and got goose bumps! I couldn't believe an actual fairy tale romance was unraveling before my very eyes! I'm still breathless as I write this.

All I can say is love is the ultimate! When you find it, don't get lazy. Don't think you don't need it. You do! I don't even have it right now, but I feel like Kat's love is part of my life. I actually feel their love, and it feels so wonderful. What I'm trying to say is don't shut love out of your life. Just because your parents messed you up doesn't mean you don't need love too. This is the rest of your life, so if you have love, cherish it. Treasure it. Never let it go! It is truly the most precious gift of all.

36

New Year's Eve

It's New Year's Eve, and I am staying in alone tonight. By choice of course. This past year was so challenging from January 2 on. It started with Karen's first surgery. Then she moved in with me. I don't encourage siblings to live together as adults. Then she had her second surgery. I got a job out of necessity while going to see her every weekend. Then we quit speaking for two months. Then Jim and I broke up. He was the love of my life for seven of the best years of my life.

After one of my most challenging years, I sit here tonight with such gratitude. I am so thankful for a new year. It's a clean slate for 2008, and it's gonna be great! I feel so thankful to have come out of this year with so many lessons learned, for the energy coming back into my photography business, and for feeling so full of serenity. I don't understand it myself. I am not sure how this happened—I've never been here before—but I sure do like it. I don't know myself right now, but I am so excited and grateful to get to this new place. I love this place. I feel so undeniably good about who I am, and what is coming next for me. I feel so blessed to have this opportunity to share my thoughts with someone who might need to look at life a little differently, especially if they have some challenges. Keep looking for the silver lining because it's there! Sometimes—okay, all of the time—you will have to create it yourself, but it feels a hell of a lot better to look at life's crap in a positive way. If I can get this far and still look forward to the rest of my life, so should you!

37

Best Friend

You kissed me and I had no idea what it meant. Jim, you kissed me and I didn't know why. I'm already sad. Don't throw confusion into the mix. That won't make it any easier to move on with my life. Why did you kiss me? Was it to shut me up? I'm sure you're not the first and you won't be the last to kiss me for that reason. I'm okay. I'll be okay. Why else would I get to deal with all kinds of stuff in my life? I can handle it. I'm a tough girl. Really. I can.

I'm going to move on once I have felt this too. I'm going to move on once I can look at a photo of you and not cry. I'm not afraid to feel this. I know I must feel it in order to move on with the rest of my life. Why else would I be here? Bring it on! What else you got?

I'd like to say I'm over it, but I'm not. But I will be okay, and that is everything to me. I know this will be behind me one day, just not today, but that's okay. It is something to learn from. Sadness is definitely something to learn from. I would like to say I never want to feel it again, and I would mean it. But that can never be the case. Life is going to have its heartbreaks, its gut wrenches, its "it doesn't make sense, and I just want to die" moments. But this time, what I have learned from breaking up is to look the pain in the face, cry when I need to cry, be with my friends when I need to be with my friends, and just look life in the face and keep on living.

I know from past experiences that the pain will subside and I will move on. I am so thankful for what I have already been through so it can help get me through this moment. Before I met Jim, I would not have been able to look at our breakup like I am. I would have completely fallen apart. Now, I realize I have had my experiences for a reason. I feel like there is a much bigger, more amazing accomplishment I am supposed to take care of while I am on this planet. In fact, I am certain of it. I know someone is taking care of me right now. I am recognizing signs that my angels are here for me. Right now, I feel this overwhelming sense that they are holding my heart in their hands. They are taking care of me and my broken heart.

I have never left a relationship before saying, "I love you" and "You're my best friend." It just doesn't make any sense to me. But I know my angels are taking care of me big time. I have just lost the greatest love of my life, but I am okay and I will be okay.

38

Lessons

I find that with each life lesson, I learn what I do want and what does make me happy. Let's take my financial challenges. I haven't been good with money. I admit it. I have kicked my shopping habit, and it feels so good to find other things to brighten my day or take me out of a bad mood. Actually, I make a game out of how not to spend money, and it feels good!

I'm thinking about money right now because I am balancing my checkbooks. It's a great reminder of where all the money goes! My relationship with money has always been interesting. I suppose my financial habits were learned from my parents. Mom would spoil me; Dad was tight with his wallet. It was confusing. Neither one ever spoke about it. Mom would always say, "Don't tell your father." I miss hearing those words. Now I get to figure it out in my own way.

I wonder how some of my lessons can be so painful—some to my heart, others to my pocketbook. I was told I need to cleanse Jim from my life—to take a shower and heal myself. This is much more difficult than I anticipated. I knew I wasn't ready to do that. I have been moving on in other ways, but I wasn't ready to cleanse him out of my life. How could I? He was the love of my life. What we had was special. Well, today I knew was the day to cleanse. I am ready to let go. Why I am crying is beyond me, but I know I must move on. I only have the rest of my life. And it's time. Time to release and understand that what we had was wonderful and to be treasured. But it was only a lesson.

Somewhere along the way, I became unhappy. I just didn't feel a part of his life. There was a huge part he never wanted to share with me, and it was too much for me to pretend it didn't affect me. I was never able to address it because I was so in love with him. Now, I realize I was the one having the relationship, and he was going through the motions. I could never admit that to myself, but the truth is coming out now, and

I am much better for it. I am a much better person now because of our relationship. I know what it feels like to love with all my heart and soul. I know what it feels like to have someone bring out the best in me. I have been so touched by this man, but I know I am supposed to move on. Something or someone else out there will take me to another level I don't even know about yet. I just need to find my own inner peace and happiness right now.

How could I not be happy with myself? This is who I am, and I didn't get to this place without trying to be this person right here, right now. And, believe me, I have worked hard on the icky parts of me. Recognizing the not-so-lovable parts of me was the first half of the battle. The second half came when I had to figure out how to change them and become a much better human being. I had to look at what triggered the things that came out of my mouth, recognize how they made me feel, and then work on not expressing what nobody wants to hear just because I want to say them. I also had to figure out exactly what would hurt people and not say it. Learning these things has led me to happy places. I never really thought about happiness until I didn't feel happy. Hell, I have "happiness" tattooed on my backside; something inspired it. I just know how important it is to me. It's also important to me to inspire it in others, and I will do that as often as I can. I know happiness is coming to me. It can be mine, and it can come to anyone else who chooses it.

39

The Cynic

I just realized I've been a cynic about love. I just thought I was okay and being real. But now I realize the things I know are the very things that kept me from wanting the next real step in love and life—committing my heart. However, I'm still not sure about marriage. Nope. I'm still a cynic, and I don't know how or who can help me get past this place I'm in right now. I've been in this place for a long time now—nine-and-a-half years is a long time not to believe in something I believe in.

I didn't know I was this injured. But maybe this is where I am supposed to be. Maybe I never could have been here without meeting Jim. He's the one who brought out the best in me. I guess now I must travel through my path and move on. It's only been six months since we broke up. We will always be good friends. Perhaps that was all we were ever meant to be. I could never imagine my life without him, and I never want to. I guess this is a huge part of my personal growth. It's hard to feel this way and not be deflated. But I know I am not supposed to feel that way from this experience. I know Jim is meant to be in my life. He was just brave enough to live through the experience himself.

I feel so raw. I'm not the first to be in this place, but it's new to me. I know I am being guided by something so much bigger than me right now. And all I can do is trust. Believe. There's got to be a reason I shoot weddings. There's got to be a reason I can put myself into other couples' happy moments while escaping from my own. I won't always be a cynic.

I thought I was in love. I thought that was enough. It was enough...for a while. Maybe now I am ready for something else. I guess I just have to take it step by step. But for tonight, I am just the cynic.

40

Angels and the Universe

There's someone for everyone. There has to be. Some try to force it on the Universe when all they should be doing is working on themselves. Then again, some people never do much of anything to make love happen. Why do they hide? Why don't they get out there and put themselves on the line? Have they felt such pain that they can never love again? Or maybe they have never felt love and don't know what they are missing. I know what love feels like, and I don't want to be without it for long. But I also know I have to feel the loss from my last love in order to move on to the next. I know my next love is out there, but I need to process, learn from, and soul search after the last one. My last love was a most wonderful experience. He brought out the best in me, and our love was real. But it's okay that it was only temporary. The Universe has something else in store for me; this I know. It was a steppingstone to something amazing, and I can't wait!

My angels have been talking, and I've been listening. I had been dating cute men lately, sowing my oats. Then all of a sudden, the men are gone. And I know why. I know it was time to make room for someone special in my life. They came and went in and out of my life so fast. I wasn't sure if I was supposed to get to know one of them. But I know

now. They were not meant to be in my life for long. These men were nice, not harmful—just what I needed in that moment.

I have come to realize I really do have angels, and they are in my head. Thoughts come to me, but I have no idea how, so I know they come from my angels. Things I just know are not my own I am fully aware are from my angels. I cannot explain it in any other way. I just know. It is the most empowering and wonderful thing to know God and the Universe are leading me through this life. I am content to know and understand this. I know these lessons are brought to me by a much higher source. That is how I know we are here to learn from our experiences.

I am learning from my debt and money issues. Those are apparent to me. I'm pretty sure I don't get to take my debt with me when I die. I work hard to get out of debt. I don't know what I am supposed to learn from the debt, except maybe that possessions are not important—just a whole lot of junk that gets collected through shopping. I am coming to terms with this one. In fact, I think I have already learned it. Now I have the debt to continue learning from.

I have digressed from love to debt, but I feel both issues are relevant. Maybe I'm writing them because it's my angels' way of getting a message to someone who needs to hear these topics combined. I just know this is the lesson I learned and contemplated today. And I also learned that if I don't change, my next relationship might be the same as the last.

41

Irony

Some interesting things are occurring in my life right now. For example, I don't care if I live, yet my sister fights for her life. I'm not really worried about death, but Karen fears it. I'm willing to take risks, but she worries about everything. I will take on whatever comes my way, but she runs from it. I face it, but she hides from it. I am seeing a pattern here.

What's wrong with this picture? Where are you in the grand scheme? Does worrying really help you feel better? Or does it just make you feel alive? It doesn't really. It will take you down. Just ask my sister. She is living it—worry, fear, running from the happy side of life. I try to get her to see another side of it all, but she won't listen; she can't hear; she's stubborn. I don't know where she is coming from, but it's not where I come from. I strive for peace and happiness in my life. We just don't get each other, and it's okay. I love her for who she is, and I completely understand she needs to learn her life lessons just like I do. Although, some of the fucked-up lessons I go through have everything to do with her and her health.

I can't believe I am about to say this, but I truly, completely, and utterly understand that I would not, could not, and never would be the person I am at this moment without the life lessons I've learned. Maybe it took all this shit to get through for me to see the shine-ola. I just got through telling Kat that about relationships. You gotta get through the shit to find the shine-ola! And I believe it! It's what life is all about.

42

Gayle

Somebody said to me the other day, "Everyone has stuff." It's true. Mine just helps me to put it all in perspective. I know we are meant to learn from that stuff. Some of us just don't learn as fast as others. I don't even know what to pray for anymore. I pray for my mom not to have to suffer anymore. But I didn't know what to pray for in Gayle's case. Is it time to let her go? Can she let go? Is her family ready to let go? She has been incapacitated for so long. So long that I think now the suffering belongs to her family.

Tonight, I told Karen I don't know what to pray for right now. She had the answer for me because she had been thinking the same way. She said she prays to God to please just take Gayle because she's not the person she was. She has very little quality of life. She doesn't know what is going on around her.

I miss Gayle so much. She was the most beautiful spirit in our lives. She was so sweet and soft about everyone's feelings. She never had a mean thing to say about anyone. She never gossiped about her friends or her family; she only tried to understand. She was the most loving, caring, and compassionate person I knew. I was twenty-five when she was diagnosed with her brain tumor. I was just becoming an adult. I didn't even get to know my sister the way I imagined our relationship would be. That is so excruciatingly painful. I feel like I am letting her go. She is in a very deep sleep, and none of us know if she will ever wake. She was only thirty-four when she fell into this deep sleep. Her kids were eleven and fourteen. I thought they would be innocent for a long time. I knew they would eventually lose their innocence, but never at such a young age to such a horrible fate. I don't know which is worse, having a loved one die, or watching them in such a futile way. Gayle had such a nice little family. Everything seemed to be going so well for one of us. Gayle actually didn't marry an addict. What a concept.

43

Journeys

I fully recognize my life is a journey. Even though love is uncertain, and my career is funky, I feel pretty good right now. It makes me realize I really don't get to choose my path. I am learning to give up control and be more of a free spirit. I kind of like this place.

I just photographed a friend's wedding. They started with love, had a baby, and then didn't stay together. I think he thought there was someone else out there for him. Then, they got pregnant again and had another child together, but he still thought there was someone else for him. He was wrong. They ended up getting married after fourteen years! It was one of the best energy weddings I have ever photographed! The energy came from their friends and family and, of course, them. I believe everyone was there because they knew—they knew these two really wonderful people were meant to be together. And now they are. Looking at the photos, I can feel their love and happiness! I felt it so much that I had to write about it. They are sooooo happy!

Returning to my journey, I feel so relaxed and unworried. It feels so nice. I just trust my gut and know I will be okay. I'm not currently in love, and a part of me asks, "What's the point? It won't last for more than seven years." Yes, I know that sounds self-sabotaging. But I truly believe in the Universe and what God has planned for me. I really feel guided at this point in my life. Yes, my family is holding still right now. I like it that way. Last year was really tough, but I'm tougher. I know this is truly my journey, and I will accept it every step of the way because fighting it is so much harder than just living my life the way God intended. I know I will find true happiness, and I find this knowledge truly overwhelming in a good way.

44

Having It All

I ran into a former friend tonight. We haven't really been friends for eight years. When she asked me about my life, I found myself saying, "It's the same as it ever was." I was in love when I saw her last, and I still love just the same as ever. The only difference is now I love someone new—his name is Joe—and it is so very nice to feel this way again. I guess there is one more thing—this time I refuse to lose myself in the whole mix of love, life, and happiness. Even though they all seem to go together, someone told me I shifted my focus when I met Jim. I let my business go. Where? I don't know. But I feel I did let my focus go. Maybe I needed a change. I know I was going through a burnout in my career, so maybe that's where it came from.

This time, I'm asking for something new. I want love in my heart and success in my career! The rest will be what it is. It feels so nice to be ready for all that is good and wonderful in life, and I'm excited to know I'm actually ready! I never knew I had to be ready for all that is good, and nice, and wonderful, and oh, so lovely. I had no idea I could actually choose happiness! I wanted to think I could. But I'm not sure I actually got to choose it like it would happen to me. I believed it, but at the same time, I wasn't sure I could make it happen. I know that makes no sense.

I'm not sure when or where the shift happened. Was it in my thinking? Was it from someone telling me I shifted my energy to my new love? Either way, I have decided to find love and success! All the rest of the really great stuff will just happen when I am ready for it...and I can't wait! Life is going to happen. But some things I can make happen, and those that are supposed to happen will happen anyway, and that's good.

45

Balance

I've definitely had my down days. How could I not? Feelings of hopelessness, sadness, and grief can be overwhelming at times, and my will to keep living isn't so strong. But right now I am happy. Despite all the sickness and difficulties. I choose to have fun, and I make sure I succeed.

I have found it's all about having balance in my life. It is so important to have fun and find the humor in life. Even when life's not so funny. Yes, it's important to feel and cry when the need comes, but when it eases up, damn—I'm gonna have as much fun as I can! However difficult the trial is, I will seek out that level of fun. No, not in a harmful or dangerous way. Just whatever sounds fun to me.

It's so important to have something positive and good to look forward to. If I don't get to have fun, life just seems too heavy. I can only learn so much in this life. And sometimes the heavy stuff is too hard to hold up on my own. Yes, I share it with my friends when I can. I'm not always sure what people can handle. I find out quickly who can bear some of my weight and who can't. Distributing the heavy stuff is also a good idea. I try not to unload on the same weight-bearing friend all the time. I might also need her to have some fun with me.

46

Burdened

Yesterday, I told Karen I have felt overwhelmed with being burdened. She has been through three bouts of cancer and survived. She was pounding me with grief and guilt. It was too much for something I'm not responsible for. I freaked out and got off the phone with her.

I haven't heard from her today. I needed some space anyway. I can't quite figure out how I feel today—a bit relieved not to have to deal with the issues, but also sad. I know our relationship isn't the easiest or most compatible in my life, but there is something tremendous to learn from it all. I've learned to appreciate her kooky self. I've learned to appreciate her shortcomings. I've learned just to be happy she's alive! But there is one thing I have a difficult time accepting—when she lays guilt on me. She knows it will work too. That's not fair in my opinion. But I know that's not how she sees it.

Karen has a hard time being real with her feelings. She always has. She fights like a teenager. I told her to grow up. I don't feel bad for saying that. But it bothers me that I let her get to me. I was really upset. It's hard to fight with a sister who has fought leukemia, colon cancer, and uterine cancer. It's very disheartening. I never know when the day may come that she could have another type of cancer. I don't want to live in such a way that I will regret the things I say to people I love. But by the same token, neither should she. But I know I can't change anyone, nor do I want to. I just want them to feel good about themselves, and how they live their life.

47

Perspective

The change in my perspective on life has been tremendous. Problems used to seem so real. Boy, have I learned what a problem really is! Most problems people can handle or find a solution to. On the one hand, I'm glad they feel they can talk to me about them, but on the other hand, they are not really problems. Perhaps I'm looking at it from the wrong angle. Perhaps the problems that have come into my life are not problems. Maybe, the stuff that I get to deal with is something very different from a problem. According to Webster's Dictionary, a problem is any question or matter involving doubt, uncertainty, or difficulty. Well, I'm pretty sure there is an awful lot of uncertainty.

How long will my family live? Will I be next? Will my family die at the same time? Lately, it seems like they will all die at approximately the same time. My dad is being treated for bladder cancer right now. It was detected early, so it's treatable. Karen's cancer has come back. It's been diagnosed as colorectal cancer, a reoccurrence from her colon and uterine cancers. A week after Karen had her biopsy surgery, we found out my mom needed brain surgery again. Simultaneously, Gayle was sent to the hospital because her shunt (a small tube that drains fluid from the brain) was completely clogged, causing advance stages of fluid on the brain. She is going into surgery in the morning to have new shunts put in. I'm thinking this is brain surgery too.

I've been trying hard not to fall apart. As I type these words, it's all too real and extremely difficult to deal with. And then Karen just called. *Oh no, what now?* I thought. She was calling to hear her horoscope! Wow, another lesson to be learned. She's facing cancer again and having to deal firsthand with my mom, my dad, and her own shit, and she still just wants to hear something good can happen in her life. God, I love that kooky girl. As much as she can annoy me, she's the most important relationship in my life. She's also the most challenging and difficult at times, but I have to put myself in her shoes, and I have the most extreme amount of compassion for her.

My perspective comes down to: The only thing we really have is our health. Once that is gone or mutated, there's not much else. Except our attitude. Wow! I forgot that I just got through learning that. It's never ending. Learning is never ending. I keep learning and learning. I often find myself saying, "You learn something new every day," and if I'm not, I get scared.

48

Christmas Wrap

I'm wrapping my Christmas presents, and as I carefully kink the tissue to fit in my shirt box, I realize my mom taught me that little trick. It saddens me to see my mom as she is now. She was always so full of life, especially at Christmastime. She couldn't have a tree without tons of lights perfectly placed. What is my lesson to learn from her? I am so grateful she is alive and doing okay. She still can't speak, and she still has a blood clot in her leg, and I don't really see that spirit in her eyes anymore. But she is still alive and I can talk to her like always. She tries so very hard to speak back to me. It makes me want to cry, but I just say, "It's okay, Mom. Keep trying; you're doing so well." It takes everything in me not to cry. I know if I do, it will only make her feel bad, so I don't. I choose to put on my happy face and smile and go on.... I know the lesson will appear one day, and then it will be so clear.

49

Man

I never knew about real love until I met Jim. It was the kind of love that when we kissed, I didn't know anyone else was around in a crowded room. The room actually turned while we kissed. I hate to say it, but it was just like in the movies. I never thought there could be such a thing. It was wonderful and so amazing! I still can't believe I got to experience that caliber of love. It is truly dumbfounding to me, still to this day. It was magical. If it had never happened, I would still not believe in such a love.

Right now, I'm in a new relationship with Joe. It's not the same as the last, but it is wonderful in itself. Maybe I lost the magical love, but I have a man who, when I am having a difficult day, draws a bath with freshly picked rosemary in it, hands me a glass of wine when I come through the door, and massages my feet while I soak. He cooks for me every night we are together, and he kisses me to get up in the morning. Yet something is missing—that kind of love I once had where the room spins and the butterflies fly.

I don't know whether I should keep looking for the one who makes me crazy with delight, or be with a man who treats me right. Either way, I am with the man I am supposed to be with right now, and he is simply wonderful.

50

Dark

I am in a dark place right now. I am finding I need my angry music. I am doing things I wouldn't normally do. I find myself not caring about injuring myself physically. Of course, it's all fun. Skateboarding, surfing, falling from the sky rides, kicking my own butt during a workout, and doing things I would normally fear. But not now. I like the idea of scraping myself up on the asphalt. Maybe it makes me feel alive. Maybe I am feeling like I just don't care. I flew to Hawaii, and normally, I say a prayer that we get there and back safe, but not this time. I was fantasizing about the plane going down and being able to help people out of harm's way. Somehow, that seemed less painful than what I am going through right now. Go figure. Yes, I am able to see this place I am in, but I still like it. And I don't see leaving it anytime soon.

Let me shed some light on my current state of mind. I have been working at a j-o-b for the first time in eight years. A health insurance agency—go figure. I have been going down to see my sister every weekend for two months. While still running two businesses (photography and Mary Kay) and teaching fitness classes. That hasn't left much time for me. It has taken its toll on me. I finally had that meltdown I spoke about in another chapter. I was at Kat's and lay on her floor. I just couldn't go back to the hospital. I couldn't breathe, but I could not get up and go back to the hospital at that moment.

I find I can't deal with this every waking moment. I would cry all the time if I did. I don't want to cry all the time. I want to have fun! I want to *live* life! I make damn sure I do have fun. This summer it's been with Kat. She has been going through her divorce, and it's been so bonding for us to spend this time together. I've already been through mine, and I have a little insight, I hope. Just being able to spend time together has been so amazing for our friendship. We have had our falling outs in the past, but this time is so fulfilling.

I am sure of one thing I am here to learn is about living life. I can only avoid how I feel so much, but I refuse to feel and cry all the time. I can't do that to myself because I would go down a path of complete and utter self-destruction—perhaps death. There are just some things I know about myself. My limits are some of them. I know and understand that living this life now is something I am here to do. All the lessons I have learned up to this moment have taught me this. Along with some other really great things too.

Life is so short, and we know we are here to learn lessons, but not all the same lessons. Each of us has our own life to live.

51

What Am I Doing Here?

Joe, you could never say, "I love you." We didn't speak to each other for four months and I had to let you go...but you came back and now you are so nice. You treat me so nice. But you still can't say you love me.... It's been two-and-a-half years, yet you still don't say you love me. But you called me and actually pursued our relationship.

I don't know why I couldn't say no to you when you asked to spend time together. I grieved the loss of you. I made myself move on. I had to let you go. Yet you are back in my life and you are so great. But I wait for us to fall back into our old ways. Perhaps this is not the healthiest thing to do for our relationship, but I cannot help it. We are who we are, together and individually.

I am waiting for us to be who we are together. You are a beautiful man, physically, supportively, lovingly. I am not seeing the man I was with four months ago. Where did he go? This is why I wait. He is still there. I just know it. So, I wait. I am enjoying our time together. You seem different this time. You are lovely and sweet. But I know you are in there. Why won't you come out? I feel very odd talking about you this way, but what am I supposed to think? We didn't work out. I have always thought that on again, off again relationships rarely work out. I still do. They are so much work that sometimes we lose sight of the love and happiness we once shared. Yet I go back to...you never could say you love me. And now I have to wonder...what am I doing here?

I do feel love for you. I do love you. You are wonderful. But how can a relationship grow when one of us can't say the word? Now, I don't say the word. This goes against everything about me. I am a passionate person, and I love to love! I want to love. I want to feel love. I want someone to know how they feel about me. I want someone to know how I feel about them. Until this happens, I will keep searching for love. But for now, I will live in the moment and enjoy what I'm feeling, which oddly enough is love.

PART III

LOSING FAMILY

52

Never Been Here

I've never been here before. My sister Gayle just passed away, my sister Karen is in chemo, and I think I just let go the nicest man I've ever been with. I don't even know why. Perhaps because I've never been here before.

I've been writing this book for so long that I started thinking I would never have to write this chapter, but here I am. No. I don't know what I'm doing. But based on everything I have already written, I know that's okay.

Let me back up to February 9, 2010. I got a call from my brother-in-law Dan. He told me Gayle was going down. His exact words were "It's hit and miss, and it doesn't look good." I packed my bags to go see my sister one last time. I wanted to support Dan, the man who has taken care of my sister for almost seventeen years.

As I left Santa Barbara, a storm was clearing. As I drove down the coast, all I could see was blackness from the storm. I thought, *Why am I driving toward the storm?* But I kept going. I kept talking to friends and family on my phone. Then I hit Los Angeles traffic and stopped moving. I called Dan to see what was going on, and he told me Gayle was gone. "Oh no!" I cried. "Are you okay?" I knew Gayle was okay. I just wanted to make sure Dan was okay. He was so distraught. This wonderful woman he had taken care of for so many years was gone. He said it was horrible. I wasn't expecting that! I somehow thought it would be peaceful. After all these years of suffering, I thought it would be easier, but she fought until the very end. She fought for her very last breath. Only now am I truly processing her death and what it meant to be there.

As I sat in traffic, unable to go anywhere, I told Dan I would take care of the phone calls. My first call was to my dad. Never in my life did I ever imagine I would have to make that phone call. "Dad, Gayle just passed away" was all I could say. He repeated my words and started to sob. It was horrible to have to tell my dad his firstborn child had just died. I think I handled it better then than I am right now. This is truly more difficult than anything I have ever dealt with so far.

As I made more calls, I noticed an amazing thing happening. As I kept inching toward the darkest sky I have ever seen, the most beautiful sun was setting behind me. I kept thinking, *Why am I driving away from the sun?* I soon found out why. As the sun set, a dark cloud on the horizon was the end of the storm; it was a line in the sky. As I was talking to my sister-in-law, there it was—the most intense rainbow I have ever seen! It even turned into a double rainbow! It was crazy beautiful! The sky was so black behind it, and it was so dark and intense in color. It was like no other I have seen before. At that moment, I knew it was Gayle letting me know I was going to be okay.

As I continued on my way, the traffic was relentless. I knew I was coming up on The City of Hope exit, where my sister Karen was at that moment. I just got off the freeway and spent the rest of the night with Karen. I truly believe Gayle led me there. I wasn't supposed to be there for her passing; she would have waited for me if I was. We had always known this day would come, but I never imagined how I would feel, act, or behave. I think Karen and I both knew we couldn't release all our emotions right then. Karen was back in the hospital with a reoccurrence of colon cancer. It was too much.

The next day, I was going to meet Dan and help him through the funeral planning. I had never done that before, but I guess I was there to be his support since he had never done it either. I woke up early that morning and had extra time. I decided to drive down to the beach where I grew up. I parked and watched the waves. They were pretty big that day. Somehow, I found comfort in my beach that I had played on in my youth. As I drove off, I turned on the radio. The song that came on—Mariah Carey's "One Sweet Day"—was a song from my sister sent straight out of heaven. Carey sings about how she knows her loved one is shining down on her from heaven. Holy shit! I couldn't believe it! I knew at that moment Gayle was with me and always would be.

As for letting go of the nicest man I have ever been with, I'm not sure about anything right now except that I am unsure. I have never experienced the death of a sibling before, so if I act a little odd, possibly it's because I am processing life and death. Maybe I will know more later when I feel better. Maybe I just endured a life-changing experience. I know I am a little out of sorts. This is a new place—one I have never experienced before.

53

Learning

Learning about Karen's chemotherapy treatment is never easy. She just called to tell me the doctor said if she didn't take the treatment, she would die a slow, painful death. All she wanted to express to him was that she was scared. She started to cry and feel sorry for herself. I told her she is allowed to do that, but the only thing she has control over is her attitude. If she becomes negative, I don't think her willpower will be strong enough to fight the disease.

Now I sit here without emotion. I feel numb, like I don't want to feel. I'm not sure I have control over it. When she started crying, I was being strong; I was in the moment. I cannot imagine what it feels like to have a death sentence. A long, drawn-out one, but ultimately, a sentencing. We all know we have to die, but we assume it will be when we have lived a long and fulfilled life. Not at forty-nine. The rest of us don't even have to think about it much, except when our grandparents or other elderly relatives pass on.

I don't think it's fair that my sister should have to bear the weight of this herself. I am willing to step up and feel the sheer horror of knowing this could be the cancer that takes her life. There's no denial here. I cannot take that chance. If she doesn't survive this time, have I done everything I could to make her feel loved and supported? If I told her to fight, it was for my own selfish reasons. I need her to stay on this earth! We've already lost Gayle. I can't bear to lose Karen too.

However, I think God gave us a substitute sister when my brother married Lari. She is an awesome sister-in-law and friend. She has been such a great addition to our family. Strong, loving, caring, understanding, and supportive. I feel like she's been here all our lives. She was a special surprise. I never thought my brother would become the man he is today, let alone find a wonderful woman like Lari. I think she is God's way of lessening the pain.

54

2010

Drain kidney bags. Check. Change pads from leak. Check. Suck contents from my sister's stomach. Check. Today, I am helping take care of Karen. Her system is slowly shutting down, and we are all doing our best to take care of her and ourselves and to keep it positive, real, and loving. It is only three months since Gayle passed away. I have felt for a long while that my family would die close together, but not this close. This is so unimaginable to me.

We just buried Gayle in February, and now it is May. 2010 is now an unthinkable year. 2007 sucked, but it pales in comparison to 2010. Karen is dying—right before my eyes. She is skin and bones. She is either nauseous and throwing up, or we are sucking the contents of her stomach. The cancer has taken over, and it is winning the battle. That is so hard to say, but it's part of my new reality.

I cannot believe I will have to live the rest of my life without Karen! I would scream it, but it doesn't change anything. She is the one I talk to every single day. How is this possible? I have never tried to imagine it because there is no point. Why live it when it is not happening? It is happening now, but before it was not, and I chose to live in the moment—to be alive with my sister, even if that meant keeping it real. Sometimes, I was way too real, but I wouldn't, couldn't, and refused to live anywhere but in the present. Isn't that what sisters do—keep it real?

55

Feelings

I'm finding that lessons can and will be learned until the very end of life. Karen is on her deathbed, yet her boyfriend Todd can still manage to wake her from her sleep and hurt her feelings. I was sitting there the entire time, so I know what he said should not have hurt her, but it did. Isn't that what matters? Someone's feelings got hurt. I saw Todd jump at the chance to fix his wrong, even though what he did wasn't a bad thing; he was just being silly. He jumped at the chance because he knows he doesn't have much more time to right the wrongs, to say "I'm sorry" to the woman he loves.

Why don't we say we are sorry when we feel it? Ego? Pride? Stubbornness? I know I have my own moments of not saying "I'm sorry," but when we know someone is dying, we know everything that comes out of our mouths may be the last thing our loved one will ever hear. What if we lived each and every day of our lives like that? How would we speak to our loved ones differently?

I know this very huge life lesson will change my life forever. I know I'm not the first, nor the last to watch a loved one suffer, but I know I will never be the same. All the lessons I have learned up to now, that I don't always remember in the heat of the moment, will become much more recallable. My loved ones will never know what I really think because it is all so trivial. What I will remember is to say the things I love about them. How much I love them, how much they mean to me, how great I think they are. The other stuff doesn't really matter. And if it does, then they shouldn't be that close to me in my life. They can be in the outer circle. The inner circle is way too important to me to let in those who are only in it for the "party." If you don't bring out the best in me, then I don't have a lot of time for you in my life.

56

Watching You Die

I can't believe I have to live the rest of my life without you.
I can't believe I am sitting here watching you die.
I drink wine, but I feel sober.
I can't imagine the rest of my life without you.
Your pain is unbearable. And so hard to watch.
We numb you. You want to live.
But your body is done.
You are skin and bones. You are starving to death.
Cancer is consuming you, and your kidneys are shutting down.
But you are a fighter.

You want to live!

You have a son who is becoming a man. He wants you to witness his wedding.

He and his fiancée just had your first grandchild.

You are supposed to help raise her. She is why you live!

I will learn from this for the rest of my life.

This will impact how I spend the rest of my life.

I will note the regret, but move on.

I will be sad forever, but will inspire smiles because that's what you always do.

Life will never be the same.

I will always wait for your call.

I will always hear your voice, your laugh, your smile, your energy.

I know God and my angels are guiding me through this life like never before.

My faith has grown even though it was weak.

57

Inevitable

May 28, 2010 was the day Karen finally said, "I don't want to do this anymore." I don't blame her. I couldn't have fought her battle the way she has. The cancer has finally won and taken over her body. She is nothing but skin and bones. I've never seen anything like it. That she had the will to live up until now has been the most amazing and incredible thing to me. I'd rather call it her will to live instead of a battle.

It seems more appropriate for Karen. She wanted to live so much, so badly, with her zest for life! Her son Travis just had his first baby, her first grandchild, on March 31—it was her reason to live. She also didn't want to leave her son without a parent since his dad Jim committed suicide seven years ago.

I never tried to prepare myself for this moment because I knew it would be impossible. Yet I knew it was inevitable, so I lived to make sure I wouldn't live with regret. I'm not sure I was successful. I wish I would have been more, done more, lived more, and had more fun with Karen. I'm guessing such feelings are typical, but I knew better. It was hard for me to do so, even though I spent time with her. Now I feel like I didn't appreciate the time I got to spend with her. We are sisters, and we acted like sisters. We talked on the phone every day unless she was mad at me or wanted to teach me a lesson. Then I would teach her one right back. She always lived in fear, and I would try to get that out of her head. She would teach me how to have fun. I learned that lesson well. But now I am faced with my greatest lesson of all. How to live the rest of my life without her. I find it profoundly gut-wrenching and truly difficult to grasp this concept. I simply cannot believe we are here. Twenty years ago, I gave her my bone marrow. And now, twenty years later, I am saying my goodbyes. I keep telling her to be fearless and look for her angels. They will guide her and take care of her.

My sadness is overwhelming. I am dealing with this the only way I know how. With humor, love, compassion, and strength. I have grown in the compassion area; that's for sure. Although it's not hard for me, I just feel like she needed me to be strong for her and to push her when she felt weak. I don't know, but I feel like it was and is the right way for me to be. But we are well past me pushing her. From the moment I arrived, I have only brought my humor and compassion to the table, leaving all sisters' bullshit at home. I am here, and I am present in the moment. This is her time, not mine.

58

Imagine

Every song has a new meaning. I can't just hear a song and think what I use to. Nothing will ever be the same. Karen, I witnessed your last five weeks of life. I showed up with only compassion and love. For the first time in my life, that's all I had to give. Love. Compassion. Strength. I had never been that for you. Strength, yes. But not compassion. I could only be the person I knew how to be. Now it's all changed.

Now you have made the biggest change in all our lives. You are gone. And I can't believe it. I knew this time would come, but I knew there was no point in trying to imagine it. I knew it would be everything it is—painful, horrible, sad, difficult. And, oh, so hard. I had to learn how to do things I never wanted to learn, like drain your kidney tubes, empty the contents of your stomach, clean your body, roll you so your bedsore wouldn't get worse.

I am going through the process. I started with regret. That one sucks. It could be the worst one. I can never bring back the time I got to spend with you—shopping, eating, laughing. Even though I always knew you wouldn't live forever. Nobody ever does. You were my sister. My confidant. My best friend. You knew everything about me. You knew all my secrets. You knew how to push my buttons. You knew how to make me feel better. You knew how to cry with me. Even though we didn't do anything perfect together, at least we knew how to get through things the way we knew how.

I'm not sure how to go about the rest of my life, but I do know you will be with me the whole time. I know you will answer the questions in my head. I know you will be here with me when I cry. I know you will be here with me when I succeed. I know you have my back, even though you are gone. There are no words to express how truly profound this experience is for me. None.

You finally passed away on June 7, 2010. I don't know whom to call when I have a problem. I now understand how much you affected my life. I know what you meant when you said I would miss you when you were gone. This is tremendous pain. It cannot be imagined. At least not by me. I couldn't and wouldn't even try. I knew there was no point.

The hardest part is knowing I will never have a sister like you again. We were the kind of sisters who could banter and love and give and give advice and go on without blinking an eye. I know there were times when we each affected each other more than we meant to, but we would always find a way to move on and forgive and love like it had never happened.

My life will never be the same without you. I will always try to find someone to be sisters with, but it will never be the bond we shared. I feel like I am starting over. I am looking for new sisters. No one will ever take your place because only we share what we shared, and that's that. I can't believe I am here, even though I knew this day would come. It is so much harder than I could ever imagine, even though I never tried to imagine it. I miss you already.

59

Karen's Eulogy

Karen was born in Chicago, Illinois. She had an older sister, Gayle, and soon after, a baby brother named Bobby. Our parents, Gerrie and Bob, moved them all to California where they grew up in Huntington Beach and had one more child, Linda (me). Karen was a great sister to us all. She taught us to laugh, live, and have fun. When she arrived, that's when the party began! Her smile lit up the room. Her sense of humor created laughter. She was kooky. She was wacky. But yet we could all see through her shield of funny. She had a heart of gold. It would shine right through that shield and everyone could see it. She was a giver. She was always giving gifts and couldn't always wait until a birthday to give them. She was a believer. She believed in God and His angels. She always knew they were watching over her. Even when she was challenged with some of the most difficult health issues I've ever seen, they were with her.

Karen married Jim in 1984. They had a son and named him Travis. What a beautiful family! Fun family trips and outings were abundant! Everything was going according to plan.

In 1990, Karen was diagnosed with leukemia. This was a truly harsh punishment for doing no wrong. She showed us how to be a survivor. She set an example of how to handle an illness for us all to learn by. She didn't complain. She would always ask you how you were doing with a smile on her face instead of wallowing in her own illness. At the holidays with our family, Karen would usually have to work at Vons grocery store, so she would arrive late. We would be eating by the time she could get there, and the first thing she would do is go around the table and kiss and hug everyone to make sure they felt her love before she would sit down to eat. She was always a kick in the pants, and we would all be laughing at her antics. Thank God she survived the leukemia because we got to spend another twenty years with her crazy sense of humor and fun, quick wit!

About eleven years later, she was diagnosed with colon cancer. And then uterine cancer immediately following. Somehow, her angels were working overtime and taught the doctors how to fix her up and get her living again because that's what she loved to do—live! And that's when I realized how to go on and live life in spite of all the adversities that cancer can create. I watched and learned. She actually made it look easy. Yeah, there were times when it wasn't so great—when it was hard and painful—but she wanted to live. Her will to live was so great that she went on to live another nine years. There were times when I saw her spirit soar when it wanted to give up. She would always turn to laughing instead of crying, and there was so much beauty in her laughter.

In 2007, the cancer came back with a vengeance. *She* was still stronger! *Her* will was greater! Even though the doctors removed vital organs, she figured out how to live without them. Once again, she wanted to live! She wanted to see her son grow up and have a family of his own. She couldn't wait to be a grandma! When Travis and Maddie announced they were having a baby, it was music to Karen's ears! She started shopping and planning how to help raise that baby.

The day Kayden was born, Karen was at The City of Hope. She wanted to be at the birth so badly. I told her I would take photos and get them to her the same day, which seemed to satisfy her eagerness to hold that precious gift. Soon after Karen was released from the hospital, she met Kayden. What a most wonderful day! It was love at first sight! Even though Karen only got to know Kayden a short while, it was a lifetime of wisdom transferred from grandma to grandchild. Karen rose to the occasion whenever Travis and his family came to visit, still having her sense of humor and love now pouring from the shield she once held up to hide her heart of gold.

When times got tough, her friends got tougher. In the last few months of Karen's life, she wanted to live, even though the doctors didn't think it likely. That is when her friends stepped up and wanted to help out a friend in need. The outpouring of love and financial support was overwhelming to Karen and her boyfriend Todd. People they didn't even know wanted to help and sent checks in the mail. This brought Karen and Todd to tears daily, and they couldn't believe that friends and strangers alike wanted to help them. They were truly humbled. The support they received brought some of the most compassionate people into our lives, and because of that, our lives will be changed forever.

Today, I am here to tell you that even though we lost our other sister Gayle only four months ago, I am equipped to get through this moment in life because of what Karen taught me. Laughter, humor, and being silly, goofy, and sometimes wacky can and will get me through truly difficult times in life. Her giving spirit that loved to live will live in my heart forever. And even though I can't imagine how I will live the rest of my life without them both, I know I will still laugh, love, and have a sense of humor through it all. Because that is what Karen taught me.

60

Human Connection

Being sick will change you and everyone around you too. If it's your family member, it will be everlasting. It's a profound experience, and any emotion can happen and most likely will. Fear. Love. Sadness. Anger. Witnessing amazing acts of kindness. Shocking and unsupportive behavior from your closest friends. It all comes, and everyone in the room will either suck the air out of it, give their hearts, or become a stabilizer, at any time, at any moment, on any given day. And the reality is that life is happening and will happen. And the only thing you can do is show up. Show up with love. Show up with compassion. Show up with a positive attitude. It's not about you. Leave your own baggage at home. There is no room for it when someone is fighting for their life. The person whose life is on the line is the one who gets to fear, be angry, love, and experience all the amazing acts of love, compassion, and kindness from everyone surrounding them in their own time of need.

While I watched my sister pass, my mom dying, and my other sister living mentally incapacitated, I learned some pretty enormous lessons.

I learned things about myself that made me proud, things that made me sullen, and things I never wanted to learn at all. I never wanted to learn how to pump my sister's stomach so we could keep food and nutrition in her body long enough to absorb something just to live a little longer. I learned how strong I am on the inside. I just show up and give my compassionate heart. Even though I may be sassy to keep it real, I make them laugh and make sure they don't sense any fear in me. Somehow I knew that was important to portray.

Some people learn how to awaken their spirits. I've seen people step up and do fundraising to help support a family. I've seen people show up to a humongous yard sale because I asked them to. The sale was to raise money to buy Poly-MVA. Karen believed it was extending her life. Our dad supported her in buying it for a while, but then he stopped. She was sent home from The City of Hope with the instruction to go home and call hospice. She did. It was too late for the Poly-MVA to help her.

All I know is my lessons are my own. I can only hope they inspire you to seek compassion when someone is in a time of need. Give your heart when someone needs love. And find your own lessons in life. They are out there. In this new world of technology, constantly looking at our cell phones, and checking social media and emails, we need to have a human connection. It cannot get lost in the shuffle of mobile devices and computers. We all have to stay connected on the human level. Perhaps this is why we have sickness—so we don't lose that human connection.

61

Gone

Karen, I want you back. I want you back! I want you back! But you are gone forever. And I can't even fathom that word right now. Forever. I just can't. I knew this wave of grief would come, but I didn't know when, how, or what I would feel. We became so close. You were my best friend, and I simply cannot accept that you are gone right now. I feel you took a piece of me when you left. My heart feels broken. I can't believe it...you are gone. It is so horrible to comprehend. I can't do anything right now to make it different. And it hurts so badly. I don't know what else to say because this is quite simply ridiculous to feel. I knew there would be more than what I already felt when you were dying; that was easy to predict. I just can't believe this is the next wave. It is so hard. The realization is so huge. It is so enormous. It is so powerful. It is so overwhelming.

I know you are with me. Both of you. Gayle is just a little more quiet. Just like always. I know you are my Angels. I know you will get me through this. I know this is how it works. You died within four months of each other, and it is reality dealing with it. Karen, watching you die was so horrendous and real. So truly heart-wrenchingly real. And then you were gone. That was it. You were gone. No one knew how to help anyone through the experience. I just tried listening to my heart. I don't know; maybe it was you. You guided me to get through it for myself, for Bobby. For your best friend Kathy. For Dad. For Mom. I think that this would take more than just you to get me through because it was you, Gayle, and Grandma Lottie.

My angels are all working so hard to soften the blow. How could this be soft? It is truly devastating. It is truly heartbreaking. But I know I have been held so gently. My heart once again has been held by my angels. I already feel better just sitting down and writing this. I sob. I cry about as hard as I can cry. I am a mess. But I got through today. I got through the week. I got through the month. It's been seven weeks on Monday since you passed away. I don't even know how I tell people that both my sisters passed away this year. It's only July, and you passed in February and June.

I can remain calm. I keep my composure. I can smile. Be funny. Laugh. And not be cynical. I can believe in love. I believe this is all meant to be. This *is all meant* to be. And since I am one of the only remaining siblings left, I cannot help but believe I am here to tell this story. I cannot figure it is anything else. How can it? I am strong. I have strength enough to tell this story. But I still cannot believe my sisters are gone.

62

Falling From Grace

I don't know what I have to say tonight, but I know I've got something stuck inside me. I can't seem to get it out. I know I need to cry, but it's not coming. I usually watch a sad movie to make me cry and get it out. I'm hoping this will help dislodge it. Joe and I are breaking up again. We love each other. He is the most wonderful man I've ever been with. He treats me so nice. He takes care of me.

I don't know how to say this next part because it baffles me. I am leaving. I have no idea why. I just know that my intuition, gut, and instincts all tell me to, and it is so hard. I don't understand it, and I probably never will. This man likes to go on picnics, he likes the movies, he gives me massages. But yet, I still must go. I can't do anything but trust whatever it is inside me that's telling me to move on. I know I am not myself right now, and I could just be grieving, but I think it's something else. Something beyond me and Joe. I know I must trust what is going on inside myself and let go as soon as I can.

Sometimes I feel as though I need to grieve over the loss of my sisters as quickly as possible so I can get on with the rest of my life because I know I am not supposed to lay down and die. I know I am here for a reason.

Today, I gave a homeless man on the side of the road half of my breakfast. I see him there a lot, but I never have anything to give him. But today I did. His eyes lit up, and he quickly walked off with the food. I was so overwhelmed with how that made me feel. I want to help every day. I want to give half of my food to someone who is hungry every single day. I can only imagine how it made him feel if it made me feel that much. I drove away crying. So many people are mentally challenged, and I have thought for so long that it could be any one of my family members. It could be anyone I love who just couldn't get past a death, a drug choice, or an abusive situation. Who knows what the trigger is. I don't.

So, I will live with the utmost compassion. Today and every day. I'm just glad I have learned to grow my compassion. It seems so important to me now more than ever. Even though my heart feels obliterated, I still feel as though my lessons are shining through. A broken heart actually sounds good right now. I know another love is on the horizon, but losing my sisters so close together feels like there is nothing to fill that void—ever. I can never replace them. They can never be replaced. I have known them all my life. I can never do that with anyone again.

This breakup with Joe has been even harder because the one person who I want to call the most is Karen. She would understand, say the right thing, and make me feel better. Even though I could never let her know that, it was so true. That's what sisters do. We make life easier, harder, challenging, loving, whatever is the opposite of what the other needs. But maybe we secretly know deep down inside it's what the other needs the most. Love. Compassion. Challenge. Understanding.

But Karen is gone. And it is so hard for me to fathom. She is gone. I never get to call her again—ever. We talked every day! And now she is gone. She was my best friend. Why was it so hard for me to be kinder, softer, and easier to get along with? Was I trying to be the strong one, to teach her how to be stronger? Only I can answer those questions. I wasn't always patient, considerate, or nice. I could have done it so much better. Had I known how I would feel right now, I would have been so different. I would not have wanted to feel this way, and I would never want to make my sister feel bad either. I am falling from grace, and it feels like a long way down. But it will be okay; this is what I am here to learn.

Sometimes I forget that someone else might read this, and then I remember that's why I'm writing this. We are all human and so far from perfect. Grace is an act—an act we should all strive to perform at least once a day.

63

Same Family

I just figured out why I felt like crying tonight. I fucking lost my best friend. My confidant. My nemesis. The person who annoyed me most. The sister who knew me best.

I have no idea why exactly I am crying tonight, but a lot of little things have been bothering me. When this would happen, I would call my sister. She knew me. She knew exactly what to say. She would support me, side with me, and tell me what I wanted to hear. She knew me so well, like she was raised by the same family.

I think this is build-up. And there is no one to take her place. No friend can handle the job. They all have their own families to take care of. I need my own family to take care of me. And there are nice familiar friends who know what I have lost. And I know they are gracious and want to help as much as they can. But there is no one, so far, who can take the place of my sisters. No one. My sisters had the same parents I did. They are women, and I cannot tell you how hard it is to live the rest of my life without them. And I will be the first to say that this really sucks! I really am feeling a pull to move away, but I don't know if I'm feeling emotional or hormonal or just downright sad again. At this point, I have no idea. I feel like I am in a place for my heart to feel love again. I feel like I am ready to take my business to another level. And then I feel like this heavy weight comes over me when I am feeling like I am ready to move on…and it makes me want to cry. So I do. Because I know, if I don't, I will cry whether I want to or not. I have some really wonderful things happening in my life right now, but all I can do is cry…and I don't know why.

All I know is I can't force myself to feel before I can. Or move on until I figure out what I am feeling. Or where to go when I am done healing….

64

Changes

It's been four months since Karen passed away. So much in me has changed. I've noticed that I keep trying to be myself, and it works most of the time. I just know myself well enough to know I'm still not the same. I just know this is still so hard. I find it keeps getting more difficult. But I know I won't be here forever. Time is the only healer, right? I just hope I don't stay here for long. I want to heal. I am longing to heal. I'm just not there right now, but I know it's coming. I wake up every morning thinking, *I can't believe you are gone.* And it brings me to tears every single day. I just can't believe it. When you were alive, I would tell myself we all have to die; it's just as natural as being born. Now that I am here, those words no longer help. They do nothing.

My pain is still so profound. I know I am not the first person to lose her sisters at a somewhat young age, but I am here to say it sucks. I suppose I am grateful for the twenty years I got to spend with her after leukemia/brain cancers, and I can't even imagine how our lives would have played out if you were perfectly healthy up until you died. That would have been so different. I know deep down inside that these are my lessons. These are the ones I am here to learn in this life. These stupid fucking hard lessons that I really don't like right now!

I am hoping this is the thick of my grief. I feel like there should be somber, depressing violin music playing as I live my life right now. But there is none. Only the music I wake up with in my head or play for myself throughout the day. I don't want to stay here any longer than I have to. What else am I supposed to learn? Because I want to learn it and get it out of the way! I want a life full of love! I don't want to wake up and find myself old and then die. I want so much to have hope! Happiness! Passion! I want to be myself again! How much longer do I have to spend here?

I know I can't have my sisters back. But if I don't get to grow old with love in my heart, hope to live by, happiness when I choose it, and passion, then I guess I better start choosing them all now.

65

Time to Heal

Today when I woke up, it was windy. I felt it. They were the winds of change. I knew in my heart it was time to heal. I need to move forward with my life. I need to write this chapter and find the courage to move on with my life. The word "life" stops me in my tracks because I cannot believe my sisters' lives are done. I think of them every single day. I wake up thinking, *I can't believe they are gone.* This life is so gut-wrenching right now. I just want to feel better. Today, I am choosing it. I am feeling better today. My friend said she was "depressed" today, but I thought, *It is just sadness. It's not depression; it's sadness.* There is a difference. Sadness comes after a loss. Depression comes from not facing the loss and letting it get away. It will take its toll if you don't face it and deal with it. One way or another, it will catch up. And that's when you will feel depressed. But I really feel that depression is sadness you've never dealt with.

I have been feeling like I have been okay with my loss and dealing with and not hiding from my pain. It's not easy. It sucks. It hurts. It hurts more than I could have ever imagined. Sometimes, I feel numb. Sometimes, I feel like I'm okay. I cry. Then I look around and realize this is not me. This is not who I am. Then I know. I am in the thick of my grief. I'm feeling like I could stay here for a very long time if I let myself. But I know that is not why I am on this planet.

I am starting to feel a sense of urgency to write this book and get it out to whoever is supposed to read it. I feel like this is a direction for my grief to go. I am starting to feel like this life is not all about having fun and enjoying ourselves. How could that be the point of living? Because we all have to die. Am I to believe that all I am supposed to do is have fun? I simply cannot believe that. I am not here to say there shouldn't be any fun. I would *never* say that! Fun balances out the shitty stuff in life. And it is very necessary. But loss is going to happen. In fact, I think we lose our pets because they prepare us for losing our humans. Why else would dogs and cats live such short lives? They are our buddies, our furry friends! But they don't live as long as we humans. And we love them as much as our family. Sometimes we love them even more.

We humans are here to learn the lessons we are here to learn, to support one another, to help each other through difficult times, to love each other with all our hearts, to do the right thing no matter how busy we are, to stop to listen to a friend, to hold their hand when they cry or look like they want to cry, to watch a sad movie with them (even when we feel happy), to drink wine with them, to go out with them (even when we don't feel like it), to take care of them however we can. And if you're the person in need of all these things, do the same in return for your friend. Believe me, it feels good to be needed. So, hold a hand, walk a dog, cry at a movie, and hug and love on the person who just did it for you. You know how it feels to need another person to care about you.

66

Feeling Guided

I feel so grateful right now. The energy is back in my life! And I know it was a huge price to pay. It's my sisters—they are my angels now. They are sending such great energy my way, and it is overwhelming—in a good way. I am not so overwhelmed that I cannot handle the goodness. I feel them—their touch, their essence, their presence in my life. It is such an incredible feeling. All my descriptions have new meaning now that I am using them in this context.

I will never be clear on this one, but I just know I am guided. My sisters are my guides now. I understand it, and if you are open to the concept, you will understand too. If you don't understand it right now, maybe you will. Just be patient. I'm not even sure how to describe this feeling. I simply just know things. I trust my inner voice—my intuition. I know it's right, and I know my angels are guiding me to where I am supposed to go. I know this sounds strange, but if you do not listen to your gut and intuition, I suggest you start today! Your angels are just waiting for you to hear them. And they are not blatant. They are soft. They do not yell. They almost suggest—subtly hint. They just want to see who is listening and who is willing to listen and hear their guidance. So don't be afraid. Listen to your gut, your inner voice, your intuition. You mostly hear about women's intuition, but men have it too. The angels are there for us all! They are waiting for you to listen. And they keep trying to get through. Some of us are harder to get through to than others, and that's okay.

Today, I was supposed to get together with Joe after we have not spoken for four months. No one broke up, but it was the strangest breakup ever. After two years in a relationship, we just simply stopped calling each other. It sent me on another wave of grief. It took three months for me to swim on that wave with my head up again. It was another loss. I do love Joe, and I believe he loves me, but something was missing for me. That's why I never called. I'm not sure why he never called. But today he wanted to get together, perhaps to rekindle our relationship? All I know is I couldn't do it. I truly believe I am being guided out of this relationship. I don't know why. He has treated me so nicely. I have no real reason to leave other than I know deep down that I am supposed to be in a new place soon. To start up my relationship with Joe again would just put it off. I listen when the same message comes around more than once, especially twice! I listen because I know I should. It's my gut and intuition. They are always there to help me.

67

Enlightenment

Okay. So, this Christmas is going to be different. There is a huge hole in our family. It is the first Christmas without either of my sisters. I am not looking forward to it; in fact, I wish we could just skip it. I feel like it will be as close to skipping as possible because I have two photoshoots the day after Christmas. In seventeen years, I don't think that has ever happened! And I am so grateful. I have never been this busy during the holiday season, and I can't help but think I'm getting some help from my angels. So much wonderful work is being sent my way! Not just my normal holiday photo sessions! I am shooting everything from food and pregnancy to modeling, book covers, and candy stores! Normally, this time of year is a bit too busy for anything extra beyond family photo sessions for their holiday cards. Even those are abundant!

This is 2010, and the economy is still in trouble, so all this work is surprising. It could be my prayers. It could definitely be my prayers! I have my sisters in heaven now. Yes, I do believe in heaven, the afterlife, a next life, spirits, angels, and God. I hope you don't mind. You may have any set of beliefs you wish. I don't mind. I personally believe we all believe in the same God; it's just a different interpretation you may believe in, which is great! He is the same Creator. The same Guy. The same whatever is politically correct to you. Sorry if I offend, but I really think it's all good.

Anyway, Christmas is not going to be easy. Every letter I type makes me cry. Karen and I would keep it light and funny. I can't believe that's what I have to do this year, by myself. My brother is funny too, but we both know there's a hole. And it makes us sad. It's even hard to write this. I don't want to fake it this Christmas. I just want my sisters here. That would make it okay. The same as it ever was. But it's not going to happen. And from how it's affecting me just to write about it, I will have to choose happiness. I will put on my game face and make it like any other holiday. Karen and I realized somewhere along the way that the only way to find happiness is to fake it, and in the process, we actually had fun and created the happy times we all strive to have. Wow! I didn't realize we did that until now. I just stopped crying and feel a sense of enlightenment.

68

Laughing

The other day, I laughed so hard I cried, and I felt I couldn't laugh any harder! It was the first time since my sisters passed away that I have laughed so hard. I didn't know how long it would take, but I knew it would happen again.

That's how we do it in our family. We laugh. It feels so much better than crying. I needed a break from crying, so I took it! It was awesome! And guess what? It inspired more laughing! It felt so good to laugh again that I forgot or didn't realize it was missing from my life.... Now I know.

I wanna die laughing! Seriously. I will go out laughing so hard that my body won't be able to take it and it will be done. And I will be okay with it all! I am going to die laughing!

69

Without Fear

Today, my friend told me she is pregnant! She has been trying for a year to get pregnant, so it was exciting news. Still, she's having a bit of mother's dumbfoundedness. She's tripping out about a human living inside of her and everything else that will follow.

Tonight, I found myself having a conversation in which I felt a bit misunderstood. I think the other person felt less at ease with it than I did. I said, "I don't think I am on this planet to have children." I have found that this statement almost always brings opinions, and at this point, I am okay with them. The person I was talking to has a child and never married the mother, which I am fine with; if it's not going to be a match made in heaven, why try? Anyway, he felt I am seriously missing something. I am no dummy. I have thought about being a mother, looked at pregnant women, and asked many people beyond childbearing years who never had kids whether they regretted it to find out if I would regret it. My answer has always been the same. I am not on this earth to have children...at least not in this lifetime.

I wanted to tell this guy about my sisters' passing and how they have left their children for me to look after and raise into their adult years. Maybe that's why I was not meant to have my own children. I don't know for sure, but it is one explanation. If I had my own kids and family, I would have very little of myself left to give to them. Maybe I'm here to show them how to get back up after losing a parent. Nope. They have lost theirs before I lost my own. I was having dinner with my niece and nephews. I am preparing myself for my mom to die, and I realized each one had already lost their own mother. And that's when I thought how lucky I was to have my mom for as long as I have. I say this with complete and utter tears in my eyes, and yes, it is hard to type, but I let the tears fall down my cheeks and onto my desk or my sleeve.

I don't do well with the "victim" mentality. It actually drives me crazy when I see it in others. But I now stop myself instead of telling others to stop being victims. Life is a journey. It's part of our entire journey, not just in this lifetime, but in all our lifetimes. And the funny thing is I feel like I am finally ready to have a child and not mess them up. I feel like I have the maturity to have a child, but I still don't *need* to have one. Yes, I know we are here to procreate. But my answer still hasn't changed.

The other day I found myself thinking, *I was born into this family for a reason*. I truly don't believe I will get this cancer that everyone seems to think I should have myself constantly checked for. It makes me a little crazy that people keep asking me, "Do you get checked?" I now just reply, "Yes. All the time." But I don't want to live my life like that. I don't think that's living at all. Live in fear! Oh, yes, that's how I want to live.... Fuck that! Watching others with it is enough for me, and I choose to live in a healthy state. You may choose to live another way. I do not.

That's just me—I have another journey to live. I am here to guide my niece and nephews to a healthy place—a place of healthy living and fearlessness!

Live it, baby! Just go for your passions in life, and find what you love and are here on this planet to do. And do it. Without fear. With pure love in your heart.

70

The Rut

Oh, not this place again. Oh, it's *this* place again! Why do I feel like I've been here before? It's a deep, deep place in my heart, and it's hard to breathe. I'm not ready to face everyday life. I feel like I've been faking it. I've been making myself go out into the real world, and I've definitely had fun. But I'm not sure I was ready for the aftermath of having fun. Although, I am not regretting it. I definitely needed to have some fun. But now I am wondering if I need any more. Normally, I would say yes. But I am not so sure right now.

I was photographing an event tonight when an elderly man fell ill. I couldn't handle it. It reminded me of my mom and my sister. I have a soft spot deep in my heart for elderly folks. There were quite a few there in wheelchairs who could barely speak. But they were there, and I found that amazing. The thought crossed my mind that someone forced them to be there, but who? What else do they do in everyday life? They have gotten so old and can barely exist. They reminded me of my family, and it made me sad. It took me back to Karen in her hospital bed in her living room. She was only forty-nine, but she was in the body of an old woman and dying. It was so hard for me to see tonight, and I didn't expect it, which made it worse. I didn't prepare myself to see these old folks. And then one of them started to fall, and I had a feeling it was the end of his life, so I started calling on my angels to make his journey through death peaceful.

I feel messed up right now, and I don't know why. I thought I was dealing with my grief, my loss, my life. I know I have to get up and move on, but I also know I have to feel it too. I don't know what I need right now, and I wish I did. I want so much to have some normalcy, but I know I can't force it. I just want to be able to identify this place and deal with it. Maybe I'm hormonal; if so, that's okay because I know it will go away soon. I do know I need to take care of myself—to be in this moment and live right now. I need to remind myself that it's only been nine months since Karen passed, and that's not very long to expect my heart to heal.

Maybe it's a good thing I want a normal life again, but I'm okay that I don't yet. For now, I will have to believe in this place I am in. I feel alone, but I don't think I would want much company here anyway. I almost feel I should be alone. Only because I wouldn't know what to do with company here. I don't feel like making anyone else feel comfortable here, maybe because it's an awkward and uncomfortable place to exist in, which is why I refuse to stay here long. It is in my nature to make others feel comfortable and welcome in my presence.

I don't want to be here long because I feel like my heart is being sucked into my chest—recoiling, constricting, shrinking. This place sucks.

And I refuse to stay here for long. I know it's okay to come here, but it's not meant to be a place to stay for long. Maybe that's it—go here when I need to and then go back to fun. This is a bad place, and I can't imagine anyone spending a lot of time here for a long period of time. So don't stay here. Go back to the happy place when life brings it. Celebrate when there is something to celebrate. Balance out the good with the stuff that happens, and live life when it presents itself. Because there are good times to be had!

Don't get stuck in the rut just because you think you should. Tomorrow is a new day, and it's always a different feeling running through your mind. The birds are singing so loud I can't get them out of my head at 11:30 p.m. It has to be my sisters yelling at me through the birds, telling me not to stay in this place for long.

71

Empty

My heart feels closed off right now. I can only guess why. It seems strange that I don't feel capable of having a beautiful, loving, wonderful, joyful, heart-filled-up relationship. My guess is it's because of the tremendous loss in my life. Gayle died a year ago now, and Karen just nine months ago. Even though it feels like a lifetime has passed, it hasn't been very long. I guess I need to give myself permission to be here in this place. It just scares me a little. To think I couldn't find, feel, or embrace love again is such an empty feeling. Sex isn't love. It's a huge part of love, but sex doesn't usually come before love. I'm not even going to pretend I'm looking for love right now. My healing is not over. Not even close. I just keep trying to move forward with my life. It is a conscious effort. I work on it daily. I'm aware of myself and my journey every single day.

Today, I became aware of my shield over my heart. I just don't know how to melt it away. Maybe I'm in this place of self-recognition because I am ready to move on. I don't know. But I do know time will tell. I do know I have to get up every single day with my game face on, be positive, keep moving, and continue to recognize each stage of my grief. I can only hope my empty heart heals in a timely fashion. I can't control the time, but I do have to look each demon in the face and not act like this is just a byproduct of grief. I need to deal with it to move forward and fill my empty heart with love again.

72

Something Wonderful

Today, I felt like crying. The first thing I did was check in with how long it's been since my sisters have died. Ten months since Karen has passed. I've been wanting to call her so badly all week. It makes it so hard to want something so basic and to know I can never have it again. I call my closest friends, but it's just not the same. They don't know how Karen and I would just sit on the phone for hours, doing our own thing, continuing on about our business as usual while chatting. It's one of those little things we used to do that I was so afraid I would miss so terribly.

Well, it's taken me this long to get here, but I am here. I do not like it here. It is simply lonely, and I miss them so fucking much. To say it hurts wouldn't even begin to explain how I feel right now. I'm almost scared to completely let go and just feel this. I'm scared of how far down it could take me. I'm scared of how hard it will be to get back up. I think I keep trying to feel a little at a time, so I don't get lost in this thing. It's grief. I know it is. I have never been here before, but I cannot imagine it is anything else.

I don't even know what I want right now. I know I want my business success back; that's easy. I can find joy in my work. It's my passion. I love what I do, and I would do it for free if I didn't need money. It's love that I can't figure out right now. I know I have been in this place where my heart is not ready or can't feel. I don't know which one it is, but I know I have been here before. My breakup with Jim led me here. I guess I just need to know this too shall pass, and I will get up and move on from here. But I have very little control over how soon it will be. I want so badly to feel fine again, but I just can't imagine living the good or bad without my sisters on this earth. I need them. I need to call them to tell them I'm having a good day, or that I'm having a bad day, or that my heart is broken. It is true they are guiding me; I feel them. I do try not to feel this way daily. I can't. I wouldn't be able to get out of bed if I felt this way all the time, and I know I am supposed to get out of bed. I know I am on this earth to do something. I'm not exactly sure what that is, but I just know it's something special. Just ask my angels.

Even though my heart feels so heavy tonight, I have to keep my faith in God and my angels. I know something wonderful is ahead of me, and I can't wait to get there, but for now I have to feel, deal, and heal from this to get to that something wonderful. And I know something wonderful happens every single day. Even today, there was something wonderful. And right now the birds are chirping in the middle of the night again, almost as if they know something I don't know...like it's going to be a great day tomorrow.

73

Special Occasion

My mom had another brain surgery yesterday. I'm trying to get her to open her eyes, so she can see me and know I am here with her. She doesn't, but I keep talking to her anyway. I've always heard that even though someone is unconscious or in a coma-like state, they can still hear you. It's just not the same without Karen when I deal with this kind of thing. My God, I used to push her down the hall in an office chair when no one was around. That's how we dealt with the reality. Humor was our friend. Now, it really sucks to be here by myself. No sisters around. No one to make light of this fucked-up situation. It makes me realize how much I need them right now.

I can't help but think about the past when Mom was so alive. I remember all the things she'd worry about; they just don't matter in the end—losing weight, keeping a clean house, having a tan, and her most famous one—saving an outfit for a special occasion. God, I wish she would wake up right now and tell me to save my outfit for a special occasion. I cannot tell you how many tags we have found on her clothes because she was saving them. And now she'll never wear them. She may never speak again. It's been five years since she has only been able to utter the word "Yesss." It utterly breaks my heart. My mom use to love to chat, especially in the mornings before I could even open my eyes. And now, I just sit here watching her, hoping she will open hers. The pain I feel right now is silent. It feels so deep that it doesn't even make a sound. It's horrible. It takes my breath away. It swells my eyes with tears and makes my head pound. It takes thoughts from my head. It makes me want to lay down and sleep for a very long time.

Tomorrow, I am running my first half-marathon with Team In Training. We have been raising money to find a cure for leukemia and lymphoma. Karen had leukemia twenty years before she passed. I'm running in memory of my sisters and in honor of my mom. The experience has been so wonderful and cathartic. As I packed up things for our trip out of town, I couldn't help but feel a little weepy. I know my sisters are supporting me. I know they will be running each and every step with me. And no matter how hard it could be, I know the pain I may feel is nothing compared to the suffering they had to endure in this lifetime.

74

Twinkle

Oh, Mom, that twinkle, that sparkle that was always in your eye! That vim and vigor that always kept us on our toes. Your zest for life taught us so well. And now it's time to say farewell. I can't believe you are leaving us. Your sparkle and twinkle have been dim for so long. It's hard to see you like this and know the real you has been in your quiet place, even though you wanted to keep on living and speaking. I know we expect to see our parents pass away, but most parents never plan to bury their children. Last year, you buried two. I know your mother and daughters are waiting for you in heaven. Look for their light and reach out with both hands, and just know it will be beautiful!

I have learned from *The Tibetan Book of Living and Dying* that suffering is a purification process. In knowing this, I know you are all in a beautiful place looking over us and guiding us to this most wonderful place. I look back on my childhood and can't help but remember the good, the bad, and the difficult times. I know we were all put on this earth for a reason, and I see more clearly every day that my role in our family is to be strong. To be compassionate. To be humorous. Look for the good and to love, even though we all have our interesting traits, whether we learned them or couldn't help ourselves. We were all just being humans. We are all here for a reason, and the reason becomes pretty clear when we get near the end of our lives. Yesterday, I realized I would want to live forever if I could experience my love for photography and capturing those moments in life for others every single day. When I have all the money I need, I will give it away just to feel this way.

Lately, I've really been having a sense of why I am here during this lifetime. I have been feeling like I am here to learn compassion, strength, and diligence. My mom is now dying, and I find it really hard when I can't call my sisters to cry, laugh, yell, or make fun of them during this experience. Sure, I know my sisters are here with me, one on either side, holding my arms and guiding me through this. But this is getting really old. Losing my entire immediate family in my early forties is lame. I want to just lie down and never get up, but I know I am not here to give up on this life. I get it! There is something more. Something else! The lessons! It can't be all suffering. It can't be all sadness! There is something so wonderful when you pay attention to each and every moment of life. Just look around. Listen. And feel with your heart. That's when you see and hear everything good.

75

Strength

Today, my mother died. I didn't know how I would feel about this day, but I feel strange and sad and horrible.

For the last six years, my mom couldn't speak or walk. For the last six years, I had to block out the good memories of my mom, and it broke my heart. Every time I would see her, she couldn't speak or walk, and it was so very hard to keep my smile and act like it was all okay. I didn't want to make her upset or sad. Hell, she couldn't speak or walk; she knew. I just didn't want her to know how hard it was to see her like that. There was nothing anyone could do to change her predicament. My mom never wanted any surgeries after we saw what happened to Gayle. My mom did it for my dad. She wanted to make everyone else happy. That made him happy, I guess. He wanted her to live. She was alive. She had no quality of life. She lost the ability to communicate her needs, her sorrow, her happiness.

I am not even sure I can express how profound this experience is. I feel numb. I feel sad. I feel like I have forgotten my mom. I had to. It was so hard to see her like that. I had to block out the good times and all my happy memories—the memories my life was built on. My mom was my buddy, my rock, my friend. She knew me from the inside out. She never messed with me. She took care of me and everyone else. I am so very sad and a little lost. We never really want to talk about our dying wishes until it's too late. After her second brain surgery, it was too late.

Mom recovered after the first brain surgery and was functioning. Who wants to go "there" and talk about dying and their "wishes"? Not me. That would mean my mom would have to die. I didn't want to bring it up. Neither did Karen. We would rather go on and enjoy the time we had together alive. Little did I know. The second brain surgery was when we never got to have any more of our good times with mom. Karen and I would make it fun and keep it light. Deep down inside, we would choke down our sadness. We would keep our clown faces on and entertain. That way we wouldn't have to cry and make it all dramatic.

The third brain surgery was a joke. Apparently, the surgeon saw something on her brain scan two years ago and was able just to test it. It was just scar tissue. This time it had to be surgery, no testing. Lo and behold, my mom only had scar tissue again. This time, she never looked me in the eyes again. She used to look at me and smile. She never opened her eyes for me again. A month later, we found out she had a yeast infection throughout her body from all the antibiotics they had been putting into her body. A week later, she had a bacterial infection. And then a deadly fungal infection had entered her bloodstream. The doctor told us people don't survive this. At the same time, we were told her brain cancer was back, in stage four, and very aggressive. The nurses were putting pressure on my brother and me to tell my dad we had to take her off of the intubation and feeding tube. My dad had one thing on his mind…to save my mom's life. I believe his exact words were "Do whatever you have to do to keep her alive."

It didn't take me long to figure out what was going on. My dad had his own path to live. He was learning from this experience, and my mom was still alive to help him. Perhaps this would be the most important lesson of his lifetime. I couldn't stop him anyway because he was the executor of her living will. I had no say, so it didn't really matter. All I knew was he had a mission, and for once in his life, he was making his family more important than himself.

His reasons may have been selfish. But I think in his mind he was trying to save mom's life. He would go and sit with her every day. He would go to lunch and then come back and leave for dinner. She was now his life. He was finally learning. And he was finally paying attention. I'm not sure what lessons he needed to learn, but there were many. When he wouldn't really listen to the doctors and just tell them a story about when he was a pilot, I wasn't really sure what was going on in his mind. But I think he just wasn't prepared to lose his wife after fifty-two years. Not ready at all. After all, the doctors had told us about the infections and how they were eating away at her brain and that her stage four cancer was back. Every day, my dad would say, "Gerrie, wake up! Open your eyes!" When I was there, I just sat there numb. I was unable to understand why he would even want her to wake up in her condition. And then it hit me. He was afraid. He knew he would have to die too. And he was trying to avoid his own demise.

Why do we want to live forever? Why do we fear death? It is inevitable. We have to die. If we are born, then we have to die. The sooner we are okay with that, maybe the sooner we will be excited to die. Well, I doubt it. Death is part of the unknown. I only know what I know about it. For some reason, we fear dying. Yet it is so natural.

When I knew my mom was dying, I thought if I could get through my sisters passing away within four months of each other, then I could get through this too. I am getting through it. But it is not the same. It's my mom. It's just not the same. Mom taught me everything that is good. She taught me how to love, have faith, smile through my tears, laugh, cry, take care of everyone else, have manners, and most of all, she taught me strength. I didn't realize all the wonderful attributes that are with me now until I wrote my mom's eulogy. It became so clear that my strength came from Mom, and even though I cry, I know I will get back up and keep pressing on to do what I am here on this earth to do. Knowing I have some awesome angels guiding me helps me keep going.

76

Angel Effort

I was driving home tonight when it hit me hard. All of a sudden, my heart felt heavy again. I don't know how else to explain it, but I just simply miss all of you. My girls are gone. Gayle, Karen, and Mom. They were the ones I want to call when life is good. That's who I want to call when life is complicated. And most importantly, who I want to call just to talk about nothing, just hang on the phone and really say nothing. When Karen and I would do it daily, she would ask me what I was doing, and I would say "Working! I have to get something done; we've been on the phone for two hours!" All along, I knew deep down in my heart those would be the most cherished times I would miss the most. And tonight, I don't have anything in particular to talk about. Nothing to complain about. Nothing much to say. But all I felt like doing was calling my sisters.

We are coming up on two years of Karen's passing. This is the month I spent watching her die. It was two years ago. I think about her every single day. My eyes well up, but I don't let my tears fall. I have to keep going, but tonight was different. I felt like I was in the moment again. I was right back there two years ago when I was figuring out how to feel while watching my sister die. I was in the moment when my heart felt so heavy, but I knew it wasn't about me and how I felt. It was about my sister and her journey on this earth during this lifetime. It has changed me. I am different. My fire and fight are different now. I am still not sure how I am different, but I am. I feel a sense of maturity...finally. The other day I was thinking I am finally mature enough to raise a child. Don't worry; I am still not ready for that. Although, I have to say, I have contemplated "What if?" What if my sisters and my mom know something I don't and it is supposed to be a divine intervention of sorts? I am relieved to say I know for now that is still not my path. We shall see....

Lately, whenever anything good happens, I just figure it's them—my mom, sisters, and grandmas helping me along the way. I blame all things good on them. I cannot figure it out any other way. In fact, I feel certain. It's been good lately. Business has been busy, my relationships are good, and I feel happy. I just miss them.... Oh, yeah. Not too long ago I put in a new lightbulb in my front porch. After a couple of days, it stopped working. Frustrated, I tried to rescrew it in, and I gave up. For a couple of months, I tried the light switch here and there, but it didn't go on. Tonight, when I arrived home, I inadvertently switched on the porch light, and it came on. I was pleasantly surprised. I knew it was my girls. I think it was a group angel effort! There was no reason for that bulb to go on; therefore, I will just believe it's my loved ones letting me know they are good where they are.

I know this may not make sense to anyone else, but I find it interesting that while I was driving home, I needed to hear from my mom, sisters, and Grandma Lottie to help me through this heavy heart of mine. And I did. I like it, and I am grateful they have figured out how to let me know they are all good on the other side. I still have a feeling I was born into this family for a reason. I'm not sure what that means, but I feel it. I am certain that one day, on the other side, this will all make sense.

77

Life

I was listening to Steely Dan on my way to Trader Joe's. It was one of Gayle's favorite bands, so I started thinking about that time in her life, and how life came and went so quickly. At nineteen, she had her first child. Instant adult. She and Dan worked hard to make it a happy home, and they were succeeding, so they had a second child. And they were happy. A few years passed and they bought their first home. It was good. Then at age thirty-four, Gayle felt funny, like she was off balance. Dan said, "You just need to work out. It's just a balance thing. Take boxing lessons." She made an appointment for months later, after their family vacation. She knew. That day, she went to her doctor. After she described how she had been feeling, he said, "You need an MRI immediately." She went. The very next morning at 8 a.m., she was having brain surgery. After surgery, she was never the same.

Tonight, hearing some of her favorite music from her past, I couldn't help but think what life was like for her back then. Back in the 1970s, before pregnancies and marriage. What were her hopes, her dreams? It hit me like a brick. I felt like I could have a breakdown in the middle of the store. I kept telling myself to just hold on and it would be okay. I did. It was. I made it out with a smile on my face, joking with the checker. All I know is I miss my sister something awful, and I wonder how my life would be different if I had her input now.

78

Human Angels

Age zero I was born. At ten, I was a little smart ass. At twenty, I was learning who I was as an adult. Age thirty, I was going through a divorce. Age forty, I was learning about losing my immediate family to cancer. The rest in between has been my life. It has been interesting, and I cannot say I would trade it for anyone else's life because I would not be the person I am today.

Some days, I don't like myself. Some days are great. Some days are just normal everydays. But some days are extraordinary. There have been days when life has been too heavy. I didn't know how I was going to get through it. But somewhere deep inside, I knew this was a lesson I was here to learn. I don't know why or how else to explain it. I knew my angels were holding my heart in their hands—when Gayle died, when Karen died, and when Mom died. And even when my heart broke when Jim and I broke up. It was so much weight to carry. And sometimes, it still is. I just trust in my angels to send me my human angels—my friends.

Recently, I was with a client and told her about my sisters and my mom. The look on her face was so hard to see. I saw the reflection of what my face should have looked like. I instantly told her it was okay because they were not suffering anymore. I don't know why I tell certain people and not others, but I found out why later—I told her something that had just occurred to me recently. It occurred to me that I was born into my family for a reason. I didn't exactly know what that meant when I said it, but she did. I tried so hard to retain everything she said to me that night. It was as if she *got* it! Like my angels sent her to me to give me a glimpse of why I was born into my family. She said something along the lines of how when I was on the other side, I agreed to come into this life to help them. It all made so much sense. I am not sure I can explain it further, but it was the first time anyone understood what I was talking about and actually had an explanation that made sense to me! I hung on to every word while she was driving me around her 150-acre property showing me the cows and one of the most beautiful landscapes I have ever seen! The sight actually brought tears to my eyes. It was majestic! How could it have been anything else? And how nice it was of my angels to bring me such awesome knowledge with such an amazing backdrop.

79

Humanity

Tonight, I walked by a photo of my mom and immediately started weeping. Later, I saw a photo of my dog and missed her too, so I started getting all weepy again. That's when I wondered how long I would miss them. It's been two years since my sisters have passed and nine months since my mom left this planet, and six years since my dog has moved on. I am sure I will be moved to tears forever from the loss of my family, but for now, I find myself feeling a great loss. I still manage to laugh through my tears, and I know I am and will be okay.

What choice do we have when we lose our loved ones? For me, it's hard to forget all the suffering they went through. As I go back through each memory, I cannot fight back my tears. I do not try. I know my tears are part of my grief. I know my grief is part of my healing. I know my healing is part of my journey. My journey is my path in this lifetime. I don't understand it all, but I have brief glimpses that help. I surely don't get all the answers I am looking for right now. I have this great and wonderful faith that has grown from deep inside of me, and I can't explain it any other way. Almost every single day of my life now, I just know there is so much more than what we can see while living these lives.

Regardless, my daily challenges occur each day just like for anyone else. My finances have been such a challenge lately, but I am quite certain that is one of my life's lessons. So I take it in stride. It is hard. But I believe—in myself, in God, in my angels. I know I will not be leaving this planet until I have figured out this crap. I get frustrated and don't get it, but I think there has to be a reason for it. I can't help but think that having money is such a burden. Life can be so simple if we live it that way. But I have much greater plans. I want to give so much back. I want to start a foundation in honor of Karen. She wanted to heal and live holistically. We both believed in a healthy and organic lifestyle. Once we educated ourselves, it made so much sense.

The women in my life who have passed make me want to make a huge difference on this planet during my lifetime. I feel like it is my job, my destiny, my inspiration, my life journey to make it happen. I know my passion for photography is related to my journey, but I think there are other avenues to make a difference. A much bigger difference. I may not even know what they are right now. It might be this book. It might be my compassion for others. It might be a foundation. The other day, the word "humanity" struck such a chord in my soul. Humanity is such a powerful word when you think about it. It's obvious where the word comes from, but what do we think about when we think about it? It's a human being human, but in an extraordinary way. For some reason, we have forgotten certain humans on this planet. We take care of the humans close to us whom we depend on, but what about the rest of them? If I don't help them, then who will? If not now, then when?

Of course, we remember if someone reminds us. But what about just simply helping out someone in need? A friend, a neighbor, a dog, a homeless person, someone who looks sad. What would happen to humanity if we all just pitched in when we each saw the need? I figure we would go back in time! Like back to the 1950s, '60s, or '70s when people cared more about their neighbors. I know we can never go back completely, but we can get back that feeling of humanity. How wonderful would that feel? If you don't know because you weren't alive yet, then try it because it felt great! It was liberating to know someone would always care about you. Even a stranger. Even people who are born without families will have another human pick them up and make them part of their own family. Yes, that sounds like adoption, but it wasn't always a legal adoption. I have loved adults who were orphaned as children. I didn't know until much later, but when I found out, I loved them all the more. Somehow, along the way, they figured it out on their own, and it made them so much more human.

But none of these thoughts right now help me to grieve any faster. They do distract me from thinking about why I was sad about losing my mom, my sisters, and my dog. Every time I see their photographs, I remember the love I have for them. It never goes away. I will always have sadness in my heart for their suffering and my loss during this life. I don't believe it will ever go away. Nope. It will never go away. But I will have times of happiness. I will love again. I will go on with the rest of my life. I just can't believe I am feeling this way right now because it really hurts so bad and feels so real. But there is hope for a new joy each day.

80

Offended

Have you ever offended anyone? I have. This morning, I received a scathing email that ripped me three new assholes. I really felt bad and still do. I cried. I responded with sincere apologies and felt terrible. I really do believe in owning my stuff. In this case, I did not mean to anger or upset this person, but I did. But she has reminded me of something important. When I have issues with people, I need to ask myself, "What is going on in this person's life that could make them so difficult to tolerate?" I also have to remember that sometimes what seems to be directed at me doesn't have anything to do with me. In this case, I think that could be true.

Perhaps I should explain. Over the weekend, I finally grieved my mom's death. I cried and cried and cried. I guess I never took the time to take care of this pain that I feel deep inside of me. Once the tears came, I knew I had neglected to take care of my sorrow, my grief, my heartache.

My mom's funeral was the day before Thanksgiving, and then my busy photography season began with the holidays—life just happened. That and I wasn't quite ready to deal with my mom's passing. Since it came only a year and a half after my sisters' passing, it was harder for me. This was my mom. She took care of me. I took care of her. We were the best of friends. My dad told me when they got pregnant with me, he told her I would be her best friend. It was a good thing to hear and I felt loved.

When Christmas came, there was this huge gaping hole at our table... and it broke my heart. It took everything in me to hold myself together, but I did. My sister-in-law Lari was so great; I think she single-handedly kept Christmas together for me that year. I was dying on the inside, but I knew we had to hold it together for now. I am so grateful for Lari. When she came into my life, I had a strange and wonderful feeling she was in our lives to help fill the void of losing Gayle; even though Gayle was still alive, we felt a tremendous loss of her presence in our lives. I am having such a difficult time coming to feel all of this right now. I feel so obliterated. I feel like all of this loss of my family is coming to a head now, and as overwhelming as it feels, I know it has been a long time coming and I need to feel it all. And as usual, I didn't know this until right now while I write it. I know that sounds odd, but I haven't grieved my mom; I just hadn't been thinking about it.

I can't force myself to grieve. It needs to come organically. Yes, it seems like something that would come easily. But once I put it off, it got placed on my grief shelf for a while. Then when something comes up, I have to take it off the shelf and deal with it. No more hiding. Just the pure feeling of my mom's loss. I watched her suffer through so much. I watched all of them suffer through so much. I can't say which I find more difficult—suffering through it or watching my family suffer through it. But I think suffering through it is harder than watching. I learned a lot from being a bystander. But that may be another whole chapter of this book—maybe a book in itself. We shall see.

Anyway, in dealing with my own stuff, I offended someone else by not realizing other people are also having their own crises that I might not know about because they are trying to be "professional" and not bring their personal crap to work. Maybe it would be nice to ask that person if they are okay rather than just assume you are the only person having this life experience. Maybe reach out and assist someone having a difficult time and offer them ways to cope. If we could do that even once in a while, we could make this existence a little better for each other. I know that's what I attempt to do. I apparently failed this time, but I keep learning because I am a work in progress.

81

Sunset Two

Last night, God made His presence clear. In my mind, there is no question whether He exists. The sunset He created was like no other! It made it clear where heaven started. People were pulling over on the freeway to take photos of it, so I wasn't the only one who noticed. I know it was God talking to me, letting me know it is all good. It was inspired by my mom, sisters, and Grandma Lottie. The four of them together must have some mighty power! I know it is their way to let me know they are whole again and they are watching over me.

82

Mother Load

Each of us has our own path or journey to follow. No matter how much we might want to change our fellow humans' paths because we love them, we can't.

All of a sudden, I find myself knowing what I want. This may shock and dismay the recipients of the love I am so very ready to give, but it's true. I love Joe! After four years of having a shielded, closed off heart, I am in love! I love this man! He is wonderful, giving, nurturing, loving, and oh, so much more! And it is such bad timing.

We broke up on the Fourth of July. I feel fairly sure I needed to grieve my mom's death. I couldn't express that at the time, but it seems clear after the fact. It's kind of how my and Joe's relationship has gone. I started seeing him when my heart was broken, and I was not ready for a relationship. That did not deter Joe. He pursued, I submitted. Four years later, he had no idea what he had signed up for—three funerals and two breakups. I am pretty sure the breakups both coincided with my grieving process. Eventually, we got back together, the first time because he called and the second because I called. This time it was different. This time my heart was falling in love.

I can't really explain the shift in my heart, but it was there. And right when it all seems to be coming to a pivotal head! While we were broken up, he met someone. He didn't tell me until we had been back together for a month. This was surprising to me, especially since all of my feelings for Joe had to come to this point!

I have feelings for him now that I haven't had before. I know they are real, and I know I love him, want to be with him, and want to share my life with him. But since he has met another girl, his heart might be somewhere else. Based on our track record, I cannot blame him. I wasn't my best in our relationship. I was selfish, guarded, careless with his heart, and I always blamed my behavior on the fact that I just wasn't that into him. Boy was I wrong.

During our breakup, I tried to move on. I also took the time just to sit and cry. I was dealing with my huge losses and grieving. I watched movies about people getting cancer and dying, about people falling in love after being diagnosed with a terminal disease. They took me back to watching Karen die, to seeing my mom in her silence, unable to speak for six years, and to seeing Gayle turn into an invalid. My heart had been hardened or turned off because it was so fucking hard, and at times, I felt I would die because of the pain. I built a mighty wall to protect my heart from hurting anymore. I will be the first to tell you that building a wall only works for a little while. Before long, you must remove the shield over your heart. Before long, the wall must come down. Before long, your heart will die without love in it. So, as I sat and cried, mostly at night watching movies and drinking wine, my heart started to feel again. I wasn't aware of the shift that was happening, but I called Joe after six weeks....

We started spending time together, doing the things I always wanted a man to do with me. And finally, this time, it felt different. I felt my heart again. I felt love in it. I wanted to talk to him about making some changes this time. About letting each other know what we need from the other to feel good about our relationship. About learning to communicate our love for each other. And right about then, he dropped his other girl bomb.

I was shocked. I didn't see that one coming! All I knew was I had to get clear and real really fast! I knew if I didn't tell him what was happening in my heart, I would regret it for the rest of my life. So, I did. Each day, I let him know about my heart and the huge shift in it that was happening. He didn't quite know what to think, and he still has some reservations about the whole thing. He didn't even believe me at times. All I could do was try to explain how I believed my heart was feeling. I told him I had finally cried and dealt with this tremendous loss in my life. And that what I was feeling now in my heart was light and love, so for the last four years, my heart must have been dead. I couldn't feel because I had shut it down—turned it off. I had to; it was too much for my little heart to withstand. I couldn't cope any other way. I had no control over it. Now I am finally ready to feel love again.

Joe understood a lot of that. He even told me how he may have broken up one of his other relationships after his mom passed away. So I know he understood where I was coming from. I know he and his sister were devastated by their mother's loss. He and I bonded over having experienced such grief. I asked him how he had handled it because I knew the inevitable was coming to me. He said they hadn't known what to do; they had been freaking out! It was a shock that she went so fast, and they were not ready for it. They went home and grabbed her clothes and lay in them, smelling her essence, and cried. They felt such a tremendous loss. Their hearts were breaking and they didn't know what to do.

Joe showed up for both of my sisters and my mom's funerals, and he took care of me through it all. I told him I will be eternally grateful for his support. Even if we don't stay together, I will always have that. I knew back then that I was taking him down that painful path again, but I couldn't change what was happening in my life. I told him he either had to support me or walk away. He chose to stay and support me. What was he thinking? Most men would have walked away at some point. But not Joe. He waited until I pushed him away. It was an argument. A stupid one. Since my heart was shut down, I always chose to run. At the first sign of any kind of disagreement, I was out of there! My heart wasn't in it because my heart was dead. How could a dead heart feel anything? Dead. Dead. Dead. I didn't know how else to react. I had no idea. I had never been through anything like this before, nor did I know anyone who had experienced anything like it. It was all new to me, and I was completely unaware of what was happening inside of me until now.

The last two weeks have been agony. I now know what agony truly feels like. It's heartbreak mixed with indecision, combined with a new light in my heart that can't wait to love again! And now I have to convince someone I love to love me back—even after four years of not knowing how to love because of my dead heart. All I have is what is inside of me. All I can do is share this new place my heart is in, and I hope it will be enough for Joe to want to stay and try us out again. For I know what is now happening in my heart. It feels so good to feel like my heart can feel again. I can't get over it. I can feel again. My heart can feel love again! And I had no idea it couldn't feel until now. What a strange place I have been in, and what a beautiful place I have journeyed to.

83

Letting Go

It's been three months since my dad died. And I am now finding myself deep in grief over the loss of my father. We just auctioned off his antique gun collection, which is what set off my grief. We decided not to keep it because it wasn't our passion, and we wanted it to go to people who shared his love for antique guns. My breathing is shallow. I have been finding solace at the home of Steve and Sam, my friends who feel like family, my chosen family. Dad was a tricky man to deal with, and I believe I learned some of his traits. Now I see I need to unlearn some of them and set my path right. I would have written this chapter sooner, but a lot happened in the days after he passed.

The morning Dad died, my brother, my brother-in-law Dan, and I all showed up to start making the funeral arrangements. When I pulled up, they all came out of my parents' home, including the caregiver. I figured they told her she could come too, which I thought was odd, but I went with the flow. At the funeral home, the caregiver got a little too involved in the process, which I also thought was strange. She was telling the funeral home director that she worked for my dad for a lot longer than she did, but my mind was reeling from the loss of my dad and all the things I knew I would go through to get over his death, so I didn't say anything, and neither did anyone else.

The next day, my brother and Dan had left and gone home, so I decided to go to my parents' home and start dealing with letting the caregiver go. She started saying things like "Your brother say I stay and take care of house" in her broken English. Then when I asked her for the keys to the cars, she said, "Your Dad say I can drive cars." I said, "No, I can't afford to pay insurance for you!" At least that shut her up for a moment. Later that day when I came back for the other car, she locked me out of the house I grew up in! I called the police. They asked if I wanted them to break down the door. I called my brother to see what he wanted, but he did not answer. So I said, "No, don't break it down."

After a few days, my brother decided to come back to help me deal with the caregiver. He arrived but didn't tell me he was there. What happened next was pretty shocking! My brother was being nice and told the caregiver and her so-called "brother" that they could take a week or so to get their belongings out of the house. First off, they were not supposed to be living in the house. My dad didn't know they were living there! My dad rarely went upstairs, and they knew it. Secondly, he was clearly not her brother; he was another nationality—I guess she thought we couldn't tell the two nationalities apart.

Although my brother politely asked them to leave, her brother got violent and started pushing and shoving my brother to get him out of the house! My brother was so taken aback that he didn't react and was shoved out of our house! Now we had a real problem on our hands. We called the police again! This time, the caregiver showed them a piece of junk mail with her name on it and my dad's address, which supposedly established her residency! Even though the cops knew better, they couldn't do anything because we couldn't prove it was our home. My dad always told us his trust was in his vault with the deed to the house. We couldn't access it because the police wouldn't let us.

To resolve the situation, my brother shut off the power and water to the house. The police called me and said that if he didn't turn it back on, they were going to arrest him! He turned it back on. We hired an eviction attorney and his kick-ass wife, the estate attorney, but there wasn't much they could do besides start the eviction process. Even that could take years, we were told. My brother kept telling the police each time we called them that there was a million-dollar antique gun collection, even though it was not worth that much, just to get their attention and make them realize this was serious.

The next decision was unthinkable. We ordered an autopsy on my dad because of the new circumstances. I still cannot get the image of my dad's autopsy out of my head. No, I did not see it, but it's hard not to go there. But now we started thinking there could have been foul play; maybe she killed my dad. In the end, his heart stopped beating, and there was no evidence of murder, thankfully.

The next day, a neighbor gave me the bright idea to put a hold on the mail because the caregiver was very interested in the mail, so I did. There wasn't much we could do until we found the trust, so we just watched from the neighbor's house across the street, making our presence known. The neighbors especially didn't want a squatter situation on their street! Finally, the cops said we couldn't take the guns, but we could photograph them. *Big deal,* I thought. So, I photographed the guns, and on my way out, I saw my dad's business card holder with business cards he had collected. When I asked the officer if I could take it, he said yes. I went through it and found four attorneys. It was Good Friday, so none of them answered their phones, but I left messages.

On Easter Sunday, I got a call from the attorney who did my dad's trust. Oh, my God, a break—on Easter Sunday! He was retired now, but he told me to call his former assistant in the morning because she knew all his cases inside and out. I did, and now we had the trust. Thank you, God!

It wasn't over yet. A lot more things happened, but I feel like you get the gist. My favorite part was how we finally got them out. I had friends come from two hours away to help us move my parents' keepsakes, like china and silver, because the police said they would escort us into the house. Even though we had the trust, they still wouldn't let us take possession of the house. The day we were supposed to do this, the police said they never said that! Defeated, we left and I bought my friends lunch. While at lunch, a neighbor called me to say the caregiver had hired an attorney of her own and he wanted to talk to me. Our attorney said, "Finally, I have someone to talk to!"

Our attorney emailed their attorney a copy of the trust and deed. Their attorney then told the caregiver and her "brother," "You have to move out." Finally! We had won! Of course, their attorney was a jackass to us and asked if they could have a week to get out. Unwillingly, we said, "Yes." It took them a week, but they were finally out—along with my mom and grandma's wedding rings and other beautiful pieces that Grandpa Louie had made. It took me a while to get over this, but it was important for me to let it go because I didn't want to harbor anger and animosity over possessions, even though it was a big loss. But nothing can compare to the loss of my family, so losing my mind over possessions wasn't worth it.

My best advice to anyone who has aging parents and has to bring a caregiver into their home is to take anything of value out of the house. I don't mean TVs or electronics, but family heirlooms and items that can never be replaced. It saddened my heart to lose the very things that would always remind me of my mom and grandma, but I had to let them go to save my sanity. I didn't want to live with sadness and resentment, so I let them go. Oh, I wished some bad things on the caregiver, which actually made me feel better, but I took no action and moved on.

84

Dad's Eulogy

Robert was born in Chicago, Illinois. He was raised by his mother, with the help of his uncles, which is how he got his Polish sense of humor. As a young boy, he always wanted to fly. He told me the story of how he put together a wooden box, nailed some wooden planks to it for wings, and pretended he was flying high in the sky. When he was eighteen, he joined the Marine Corps and served in the Korean War. When he was done serving, he started taking pilot license classes and turned his dream into a reality by learning to fly. He became a pilot for Eastern Airlines, then Western Airlines, and finished his thirty-year career with Delta. Flying was his passion and his first love.

In 1959, he married my mom, Geraldine. They had a daughter Gayle, then Karen a year later, and then Bobby a year after that. I think they thought they were done having kids at that point, but they were wrong. I was the happy surprise that came along six years later. Mom and Dad had an undeniable bond that lasted fifty-two years until Mom passed away. The last few years were hard on my parents, losing Gayle and Karen to cancer, and then when Mom died, Dad lost his best friend. It was truly a tremendous loss for him, and he struggled through it, but in the end, he started living his life again. His strength was inspiring to us all because his heartache was overwhelming.

My dad could do anything he set his mind to—welding, building a house, including anything from the electric to the plumbing, and everything in between. He was a man of many talents, and he could do anything he aspired to do. He was strong willed, maybe even a little stubborn at times, but no one could stop him when he had a goal in mind.

He had many hobbies too. Collecting antique guns was his favorite. Building replica boxes for those guns was an absolute delight for him. He learned how to do metal bluing for them as well. He enjoyed restoring cars, being a gunsmith, and even owning a gun shop for a while.

Dad was a generous man. He wanted to pay for an education for each of us, and he used to joke that his gun collection was the college education he didn't have to pay, but he would have sold it at the drop of a dime if one of his kids had wanted to go back to school. He made our holidays abundant, often with surprises of bikes and big ticket items. He would send us on trips to Hawaii, and there was always a pool party going on at our house when we were young.

When we would have a disagreement, Dad was always quick to smooth things over. The biggest, most important quality I learned from my dad is to have a sense of humor. To this day, we laugh a lot, even when adversity looms. I got my sense of adventure and can-do attitude from my dad. For this, I will be eternally grateful.

Our family is here today not only to mourn his death, but more importantly to celebrate the life he created through his unique talents and skills, which he learned and cultivated solely on his own. His drive and determination were relentless, and the lessons he taught us have helped us become the people we are today. Through these lessons, we will always remember him, miss him, and honor him with love and laughter in our hearts.

85

Turning Forty-Five

Turning forty-five was not exciting since I never thought it would be. I am now officially pushing fifty, and that sounds kinda old. I am not sure I like it either. I have learned to accept the things I have no control over. I have no older sisters to look to for guidance. I don't like that. But I have learned to accept my path. I have learned to find my other sisters out there, like my sister-in-law and my friends who think of me as a sister. God knows when to plant them in our lives. That's just how He works. He has brought love back into my heart, which is huge. I can't help but think my sisters, mom, and grandma had something to do with making this happen sooner than it might have.

All I know is I get to keep on living. I get to keep on loving! That was a typo, but I got it—while I am living, I also get to love. That is so very enormous and wonderful, and it is so important for me to remember I am here for a reason. I feel so mixed with emotions while wondering why I will be here longer than my sisters. I feel so grateful to have received this message even though I don't know what to do with it. But I know it is real. I have received it in my mind. And if that's not enough, that's okay with me. I know. Deep down, I know my angels guide me, follow me, and love me. And they never let me down. They just let me know what I need to know, on a need-to-know basis.

My life is gaining momentum in a really wonderful way. Even though life continues to happen—my only aunt, Aunt Sevie, passed away, and my brother and I were her last of kin. It was a strange sensation to have to plan her funeral and be the executor of her very outdated will, which will now go to probate. My aunt only listed my mom and my sisters as her beneficiaries in her last will and testament from twenty-four years ago. My brother and I were not listed, probably because back then, I was only twenty and my brother was a mess. Needless to say, my aunt thought she was leaving everything to me and my brother, not realizing she did not list us in her will and never dreaming my mom and sisters would pass before she did.

86

Eleven

I want to share one of my sister's fun beliefs. When Karen was alive, she found out that the number one was the sign of angels. Every time she or I looked at a clock, it read 11:11. We would say in exultation, "It is 11:11!" All the time—every day! And we always knew our angels were with us just about every day from then on.

Since Karen has been gone, I see nothing but 11s—on the clock, in the number of emails I have, the chair I ride on the ski lift, the table at an event. You name it, the 11s are always there for me. I know it is Karen saying "Hi" to me. Psychics have told me Karen is over my right shoulder and Gayle is on my left side.

Tonight, I was housesitting for my friend. She has a very cool cat, so I don't mind helping out when I can. I went over tonight to take care of Rosie. I fed her and then she was ready to snuggle up on the sofa with me. Rosie was purring and well relaxed when all of a sudden, I looked at her and her eyes were fixated on the ceiling. Cat eyes, non-moving, looking straight up at the ceiling! What was she seeing that I couldn't? All the hairs on my spine went up and I froze. I told Rosie it was probably my family, and I asked them, if it wasn't them, to please leave. The next moment, I looked at the football game on the TV and the jersey that showed up over and over was....you guessed it, #11. I was not settled so I called Joe who said just to leave. So I did, with him on the phone. I wasn't so much scared as I was stressed, like all my muscles went weak from the stress of not knowing what or who was in that room. Joe stayed on the phone with me until I got home.

When I got home, all was right. I watched the American Music Awards and a football game, bouncing back and forth between commercials. When Mark Anthony won an award, he said something I cannot ignore: "Just because you're alive, doesn't mean you're alive." I'm sure I have heard that before, but today I was ready to hear it. The last three years have been hard. I had to bury my sisters, my mom, my aunt, and my dad. Just when I was thinking that was what I needed to hear, JT comes on and sings a song about how you can't drink yourself away. I am the first to realize when I need to break a habit.... I know it will come, but today is not the day.

Today, my friends text or call me to tell me it's 11:11, and I know it's Karen saying "Hi" or that she is always near me. That's why I think what Rosie saw tonight was probably her.

87

It's Here

My dad died four months ago, and I am ready to grieve. I can feel it. I want to cry, but I can't. I feel angst. I know this feeling; I have been here before. It seems like it would be easy to do, but it's not. I know I need to watch a sad movie; which always helps. My dad died before I could say goodbye. He had a round of chemo and died that night. I was not expecting him to go so fast. I thought I would get to say goodbye. I was thinking it would be slower, like it was with Karen, and I would watch him go. I would say goodbye.

So much has happened in the four months since my dad died. Much of that time was taken up with getting rid of my dad's squatter caregiver. As a family, we united. It was liberating for our small but mighty family to be on the same page. We were definitely brought together again, even if it was in a much smaller unit—now it's just my brother and sister-in-law, my two nephews, my niece, my great-niece, my brother-in-law and me.

It also taught us that this truly difficult time in our lives was manageable. My brother Bobby and I were now left to deal with our dad's house of forty-seven years. I never thought it would come down to the two of us. Perhaps that has been a huge part of this loss. I always thought I would have my older sisters to turn to in losing our parents. But they are gone. Watching my parents lose their children was so hard. My mom couldn't speak or show emotion to express her grief. My dad was stifled from no one raising him emotionally. But I saw him cry—I saw him mourn when he lost my mom. It was so hard because I knew where he came from. He was a difficult man who yelled and swore every single day of his adult life. It was hard to hear, especially when it was aimed at my mom. Most of it was aimed at my mom. My brother too. Sometimes Karen. Rarely at Gayle. Rarely at myself.

Losing my mom was my dad's biggest life lesson. He was now confronted with all the years of mistreating her. My mom did everything for him. Everything! She never complained, just accepted. He would berate her every single day. Mom would just say, "It goes in one ear and out the other." I never believed her. I now know it went in one ear but never came out the other ear because it gave her brain cancer. Or did it?

I have seen a lot of my family members die in the last three years. One thing I know is we will all die and we don't get to choose when. Why we die when we do is a mystery. Why does a baby die? Is it for the parent to learn a lesson? I cannot imagine a worse lesson to learn. But I can only trust there is a much bigger lesson to learn. Why else would both of my sisters die within four months of each other, and then my mom die the next year, and then my aunt die nine months later, and then my dad eight months after that? All within three years. So much can change in three years—your whole life, or at least your whole family. I guess I better start finding my new family. I always thought we were born into the family we learn our lessons from, but we choose the family we want.

88

Breakup

Joe broke up with me last night. I guess when he asked me if I wished I could sing, I should have answered yes. Instead, I gave an honest answer, saying I am okay with the gifts I have and I don't want to be greedy. That set him off, and that was the end of us. As I watched him shove his massage table into his car and drive away, it truly felt like the last time we will break up. I felt my angels were holding my shoulders and telling me to let him go. Today, I am very sad and weepy. I dreamed that he came back. I also dreamed that my mom was still alive, and it felt so real. I kept hugging her and crying because I knew how much I would miss her. I woke up with that heavy heart feeling I have felt before—a feeling of dread, yet a little hope for what the future holds.

I feel like I am on autopilot right now. I want to let Joe know how sad I am, but I'm not sure if I should contact him. I am checking emails, getting to work, and getting things done. I don't feel like telling anyone; then I would have to talk about it. Last night, I called Lauren to help me through the hardest part, and she did. I feel numb, and talking about it now would only make me feel. Today, I feel like watching sad movies to help me grieve and get through this so I can move forward. I am so sick of being in grief, but I feel like maybe this time I get to move to a completely new place when I am done.

89

Compassion

Some people really have no idea what grief is. They seem to think if you just watch a happy movie, it will be gone. All I can say is "Wow!" and "You don't know what grief feels like. It is a process. It takes time." It will take the rest of my life, and I'm only forty-six. I am okay with that. I know how to stay home and take care of myself, but then I can go out and be in public and be okay with a smile on my face. I know I should not go out when I am not feeling it because it will show up on my face or in my tears or in someone's ears. Either way you slice it, grief is usually not a good experience for almost anyone involved.

I would also like to add that grief is not depression. Grief is actually healthy. It is necessary. If someone lost four of their six immediate family members in a three-year span, I would be extremely concerned if they did not show signs of grief. My best advice to anyone who has experienced a loss is to grieve and let others grieve. Don't be trite. Don't encourage them to watch a stupid fucking movie to make them laugh. It won't work because they need to grieve. That's all. It's grief, not happiness. It's not something they can avoid. It is something one needs to go through when they lose their sisters and parents in a short period of time.

Grief might be an interesting experience for those lucky enough not to experience it, but what I need you to know is this—be there. Support those who are grieving with love and compassion. Feel with your heart. Put your mind aside because it probably has too many thoughts. People who are grieving usually have enough thoughts already. I know it is really hard to feel another's experience if you have not had the same one, but try. Maybe you can learn something...like compassion.

I am feeling vulnerable in my grief. I have a tremendous need to have someone take care of me. I don't know who, besides my friends.

90

Positive Light

Now I know why people smoke pot. It's so they suppress the asshole inside them. At least that's how I feel about myself right now. It's bad when your friends let you know how your words have affected them. I think I am controlling my mouth, but apparently I am not. I am feeling frustrated right now—annoyed, frustrated, and full of angst. And the worst thing is I am not exactly sure which life issue is causing the most issues.

Am I grieving over my dad's death? Tears just started welling up in my eyes when I typed that, so I am guessing, yes. Then I ask myself, "Am I upset about my breakup with Joe?" A heavy sigh comes over me and tears follow. That is followed by not understanding what the last five years were meant to be. I have a hard time believing my life of relationships has ended. Yet I know that smoking pot will not change this. I kind of think I should not leave the house until I figure out my shit.

I know it's me. If this is how I am behaving, then I know I am around people who don't bring out the best in me. Or worse, my friends don't know how to be good friends, probably because they have their own shit to deal with.... I do have a friend who always surprises me, my neighbor who lives on the same property as I do. I can go to her with my issue and always be amazed by her answers...and they always involve God. They are the most beautiful answers. It's like she is an angel—an angel sent to guide me and help me with my shit. She always finds the right answer too. I am amazed by Christine. She had a difficult upbringing, yet she taught herself how to find understanding and peace in her heart and love for herself and others. She told me she wanted a different kind of home, but God brought her near me because that's what she needed in her life.

I needed to be reminded that I am not all bad. A lot of people really do like me and are affected in a positive way by my sarcasm, sass, and wit. In fact, I met one today. Emily really likes me. She is from New York, and she says the word "fuck" is a noun, verb, and adverb, and used by everyone in NYC. So what's the problem, right?

I guess I use my friends as my family now. Since I don't have any sisters to abuse, my dark side comes out with my closest friends. They don't like it. I don't blame them. I know I can be harsh. I don't even like that part of myself. I am a work in progress, and this is part of my progress. Owning my shitty side and knowing it too shall pass is always a positive light to shine on myself.

91

Vague

Sometimes when I am in the deepest darkness, I see the light. For the last week or so, I have been feeling like I need to have fun. And by that I mean I need to have fun! Unfortunately, that means I have too much fun, which puts me out of balance. Oh yeah, the other thing I seem to do is really offend my friends. I have noticed myself being really needy and wondered about it. It seems I have been out of balance for a while now.

I noticed. My friends noticed. Hmm...there seems to be something going on inside of me. And it's not good. It's not terribly bad, but it's not good either.

It's about five months since my dad died, and a month since Joe and I broke up. Take your pick on which one I am not dealing with. I'm not sure either, but I am guessing it's both. It's a toss-up or a double-duo of loss. I can keep going on being strong, but I don't think I will fool anyone. Not even myself now. Why am I always the last to know I am dealing with my shit?

Today, I need to be vague. And that's it...vague. I am owning my shit. Are you?

PART IV

RETHINKING LIFE

92

Middle Age

Today, a psychic told me I will live into my nineties. I'm sure you might be thinking, "That's great." I do not think that's great. I was not planning on living past eighty. That's it. Eighty seemed long enough. Don't get me wrong; I am grateful for this life and all that, but it has been a difficult life so far. I can only hope some blissful and amazing days are ahead.

Now, I have to rethink this life I am living. If I live to be ninety, then I am officially middle-aged right now. Hmm. I guess that's not very different. It's only a little longer to live without my family members who have passed on. It's only ten more years than I intended, and I better be in frickin' good health. That's all I have to say! Whoever thought this was a good idea better be right.

The psychic also seemed to think I was ready to have a child or at least get pregnant. Oh, boy. A child at this age? I was thinking a year or two ago that if I were to get pregnant, I would seriously consider having a child. What was I thinking? Then I realized just maybe it wasn't something I should decide on my own. Maybe my family, who has passed on, knew better than me. This I have considered. Then I think about how I never really wanted kids. How could I want them at *this* age? I am turning forty-six next week, and I have never wanted children. They suck the life out of me, yet my great-niece Kayden has stolen my heart. She has my sister Karen's spirit. And it is so beautiful.

Last year, I thought I was finally mature enough to have a child and not completely fuck them up. Yes, one of the reasons I didn't want to have a child was I felt I would fuck them up for life. The other is because they drain me. I was young when I became an auntie, only eleven. My mom would help my sisters by taking care of my niece and nephews while they went to work. I would only be in the same room, but I would feel completely drained when they left. Yet I hear little Kayden, with her little voice saying, "Auntie...Auntie," and I love her little voice so much that I find how she makes me feel to be indescribable, except to say she has stolen my heart.

How could I want to have a child of my own when this most amazing child already exists and has stolen my heart? I want to give her my love, attention, and affection. My sister never said to me, "Take care of my grandchild," yet my heart knows. And I will. I can only do what I can do. I mean they and I all have our own journeys, but I want to take on the role of auntie and enjoy all that it entails—love, gifts, teaching, scolding, more teaching, sharing, and hoping.

93

Essence Qualities

I wrote a letter in my head to Joe tonight. I had a euphoric run, and it just came pouring into my brain.

> Dear Joe,
>
> I just want to thank you for loving me for the last five years. I feel like my angels brought you to me. I am a better person because of you. I am so grateful because of you. The night you left, I felt

my angels holding my shoulders and saying, "Let him go." I stayed right where I was standing on the cold sidewalk, crying. It was so hard. I had nothing left. You gave your heart to me. I love you. I know my angels sent you to me because they knew what I was about to go through in my life. I had no idea what you were going to get dragged through. It was so hard for you, but I believe it has somehow made you a stronger man. I know it was all meant to be, even though it feels like a shitty joke. I am so grateful for you in my life. I will never forget what you did for me, especially when you really didn't want to. I know what that feels like, and it takes guts and so much passion, love, empathy, heart, and soul. I can't even think of the rest of the words, but there are many!

I guess my angels have released you from your duties for now. Now you get to be free and go find yourself. Just as I don't grieve when I am in a relationship, you and I don't seem to grow while we are in one. I feel so many things right now, but gratitude and love are at the top of my list. You taught me to love again. I will admit I was in many of my darkest hours, times, and places while I was with you, but I completely realize what we had was real and, oh, so scary. It was truly uncharted waters that neither of us had been in together or separately. You had experienced the death of your mother, and I remember asking you how you handled it because I knew it was coming. I had no idea it would come like it did. The last three years have been so overwhelming and sad, and my heart was breaking over and over and over.

Letting you go has been so hard and strange, yet freeing. I feel like I have set you free. I have so many hopes for you! I hope you figure out what makes you happy. I hope you figure out how to get past your fears. I hope you will love me again. You are the man I asked for after Jim. I asked for a man who would love me unconditionally, who would bring out the best in me, be fun, have a sense of humor, get my sense of humor, be balanced, happy, passionate, and find happiness in the little things in life. I asked for someone I would have great sexual chemistry with, that we would feel love for each other, have great energy, someone who would work hard and know how to have fun, have similar interests, include me in his life, and enjoy taking care of me. Someone who would be compassionate and emotionally balanced. That we wouldn't be able to get enough of each other, yet we could get our work done. I asked for instant attraction, for someone who was patient, made me feel pretty just from the way he looked at me, who was socially compatible with me, someone who was active and exercised, lived a healthy lifestyle, was faithful and loyal, knows what he wants, and isn't afraid to work toward it. I asked for someone who was independent, compatible, felt free to express himself, made me feel like a woman, could dance and enjoyed it, was strong emotionally and physically, was supportive, was realistic but also dreamed, was down to earth, interdependent, could relax, understood that life is fragile, and was not excessive. I wanted someone who was for real and enjoyed spending time with me.

I just read all those things and realize that we had almost every single one. I feel a little sick right now, like I let an awesome man get away. I don't know what to think about all this, except to let you find yourself for a bit and hope that if we are meant to be together, fate will lead us back to each other....

After our last breakup, after my mom died, I don't think Joe's heart was completely convinced that we should be together. I think his heart was a little hardened, like mine. Maybe he learned more from me than he should have.

94

Photos

Today, I was able to hang photos of my family. I was strong when I hung them. But tonight, I find myself a little less strong. I saw on Facebook that someone I went to high school with has passed away from cancer. I read the journal from her last months of life and found myself crying and deeply touched. I barely knew her, but I felt such compassion for her family and what they were enduring. Her parents are experiencing the loss of their child—a pain I can't even imagine, but I watched my mom go through it in silence, and I watched my dad, who didn't know how to deal with emotion. It was torture to witness.

Tonight, the radio station I listen to is playing all eighties songs...heavy sigh. For me, those were the good ole days—when times were good and no one was suffering. Deep breaths are helping me, and now Prince is playing—"Purple Rain." I was just learning about life back then and figuring out how to get through it. Haha—life seemed so challenging when we were young. I'm sure it does for everyone. I am so grateful for having a period in my life that wasn't so difficult. It really was just growing up and having normal lessons. I remember my next-door neighbor Beth and I went to the drive-in and watched *Purple Rain* while drinking Tom Collinses. It was a good night; she and I reconnected on a friend level after growing up next door to each other.

Every time I walk down the hall where I hung my photos, I feel different. Each time it's a different emotion. At first, I felt happy to see them. Tonight, it made me sad my loved ones are gone. I am now feeling melancholy and remembering the times gone by that can never be recreated. Another heavy sigh.

Thanksgiving is next week. The holidays are never easy anymore—at least thinking about them is not easy. It's hard not to think about past holidays. But Kayden brings new life and love and fun! This year, my dad is gone too. While he was alive, we kept the holidays the same for him because he wasn't comfortable with the change and we honored him. My brother Bobby is having a hard time and won't be coming for Thanksgiving. As much as that saddens me, I think he needs to show up. I relent and understand that he is going through his grieving process.

95

True

I figured out a long time ago not to live my life with regret. But the older I get, the more I regret. I regret not doing things I should have done while I was young. I regret not saying things to my sisters when they were alive. And right now, I have huge regret in saying something to a friend I think of as a sister. I said it with love and wanted it to help, but it didn't. It only made her face her own stuff and cry, which was when I realized the damage I had done.

I seriously damaged our relationship, our friendship, our sistership. I think I sank our ships. But I am a firm believer that I am a work in progress. I know I have learned all kinds of behaviors while on this planet. Some are great and humorous, but some I need to let go of.

In the morning, I am moving after renting this house for fifteen years. I have accumulated a lot of stuff. Hundreds of boxes of wedding negatives. My garage had so much stuff in it. I cleared out almost everything, but my neighbor still thought an incredible amount was left. I was annoyed by the comment, but thankfully held my tongue. I guess I have learned some things about moving, stuff we hang on to, and friends.

I find that you learn who your friends are when your family dies and when you move. In fact, I feel the need to write a separate book on how to support your friend when their family dies. It's kind of the same as when you move. Show up! Actually, that's the whole book. Just show up. Show up at the funeral. Show up at their door when you hear the news that they just lost a sister. Show up when they lose a sister four months later. Show up when they have to grieve the loss of their mother the next year. Then their aunt the year after that. And then their father the next year. I know this span of loss is unusual and not many people have experienced it, so put yourself in their shoes. Really take the time because when your family dies, imagine whom you will expect to show up. Will it be the friend whose sisters' funerals you didn't think she needed you at and missed? Or the friend whose parents have died and you know her sisters are already gone and won't be there to hold her up. If not you, then who?

I know I sound passive-aggressive, but that's exactly how I feel. Only now am I beginning to understand how quite a few of my friends couldn't figure out how to handle my losses, and it never occurred to them to show up and support me through it. It brings me back to "If not you, then who?" Who did you think would be there? My other friends? They didn't show up either. I realize I sound like a pity party, but I expect a lot from my friends because of what I give them. I show up. I am disappointed. I did expect more. Maybe that was my fault. I should have told them beforehand that if my family dies in a three-year span, I will need you there to support me. It sounds ridiculous. First, that I would lose my family like that, and second, that I would have to ask.

Somehow, this all ties back into my regret, my disappointment, and my loss. I guess it's all about me. That's all it really is. My feelings, my grief, my emotions. Perhaps no one can relate because they have never experienced it.

I do have a friend who showed up every time. Leslie showed up to every funeral, and twice to help me move from two hours away. Leslie, I will always know you are a true friend, and I am humbled. I know my friends showed up the best they could given their circumstances, and it will all be healed one day. At this moment, I have a hard time thinking I will show up when their immediate families die. I know—vindictive. I can't help it. Where were they? I am still hurt. I don't know how long it will take—only time will tell—but because I know about this thing called regret, I know I need to let it go. And I want to because otherwise it will only make me passive-aggressive to those I love.

I have friends showing up tomorrow, and even though I wish they had supported me through loss, I have to remind myself they are showing up when I ask them to...though it is also hard for me to have to ask and part of the emotionally crappy frenzy I create in my head. Ugh. It's not easy being me.

96

Dear Mom

Dear Mom,

It's been two-and-a-half years since you passed. I miss you each and every day, and I can't believe how much I have learned even since you've been gone. Your great-granddaughter is so smart and fun and beautiful. The spirit of her grandmother, your daughter Karen, is in her, and that is so much fun! Her sister is on the way. I can't wait until I get to teach them everything you taught me. Strength, love, a giving heart, and compassion will be my favorites to teach them.

I know that when we were young, you took our interesting journey and turned it into the best experience possible. I was the youngest and most protected. For that, I will be eternally grateful. I always felt like you were my best friend. My siblings were older, and I was kind of like an only child, so you were my confidant.

You cried when you dropped me off at college. You smiled though your tears. And you supported me in all my endeavors, even though some of them scared you. You would always ask me if I was scared to do the things I would do on my adventures. I would smile and say, "Why would I be scared? It's going to be fun and empowering!" I think you even felt empowered.

Your heart broke when you buried your two eldest daughters, four months apart. It was easy to see. You couldn't speak or walk because your own brain cancer took your cognitive functions from you. And I stood by you, just like you taught me—to be strong, to use my inner strength with all my might, to be the woman you raised me to be. And I am here to say that is who I have become.

You passed away a year and a half later. Your body succumbed to brain infections, and I watched you go. I knew you were gone. Dad tried to will you to stay because he wasn't ready. It was clear he wasn't ready, but you stayed as long as you could to help his journey in losing you. It was hard to witness.

Dad died less than a year and a half after you. He tried to make a comeback and was doing pretty well, but I think his heart couldn't take all that he was dealt and it finally gave up. I know he is with you and my sisters now, and you are holding hands, swinging your arms in heaven.

The strength you taught me by example carried through, and I wrote all of your eulogies and stood up as if I were you. I smiled even though I wanted to cry. I love with all my heart. And I laugh as much and as often as I can. Even though I miss you every single day, I am grateful for all the wonderful gifts you have left me with so I can go on with the rest of my life.

You were my buddy. My best friend. My mom. I surround myself with photos of all of you to make me feel like you are only two hours away, but in reality, I know you are with me always. You are all my angels now. Guiding me through what is to come next in my life. And I never have to worry…that was your job. And even though it's truly hard to go on and live my life without you, it is a little bit easier knowing that what you taught me will carry me through and I will be all right.

I love you, miss you, and don't know how to end this letter.

Love,

Me

97

They're Gone

I can't believe I have to live the rest of my life without my family. It's been four years now since my sisters passed.

I have been going through a shift lately. I am not certain what it is, but I know it's there. It's vague. It's real. It keeps me guessing. But I know it's there. What is it? I don't know for now, but I do know that when I went to bed, all I could think was that my sisters and parents and aunt are still gone. And every single day, I need to talk to at least one of them. Until now, I have been telling myself that they can hear me and they are here, and I truly believe that. But what I need is to hear them, see them, feel them.

I am not feeling like myself. I know I need to surround myself with my friends, who are real and who know what real-life situations are like. It helps anyway. They feel like my chosen family. They don't judge. They don't do anything but help me through when I feel like this. I don't know if I can explain it, but I know who to turn to when I feel out of sorts.

For a while now, I have been feeling different, like my head is in a cloud, and I can't really focus my energy to get work done. I couldn't put my finger on it, but tonight, I know it's my family. Tonight, I feel the loss of them. I feel a certain empty feeling that I thought would be gone by now. And it was, but it has returned…only leading me to believe the process goes on and on…I am guessing for the rest of my life. I always said it would, but now I know for sure.

My eyes were feeling cloudy for the last few days…but now they feel more clear, and I am feeling like I can see again. My heart feels heavy, but my eyes know. It is a difficult place to be, but I know I will be in a new place soon—maybe with love in my heart.

98

Glitter

We are finally not burying our family; we are growing our family. It warms my heart so much, but it also leaves it feeling a little empty. My nephew just had his second daughter, and I just found out my niece, Gayle's daughter, is pregnant.

It is the middle of December, and the holidays are hard again. They just remind me of my family and make me miss them so much. The music in the stores still causes me to almost fall apart, but I don't. I'm reminded that I should be talking to my sisters every day, figuring out what gifts to buy, but I can't. It takes me a little while each year to figure out why I am not a super-happy person, but then I do. And I give myself permission to just feel where I am right now. I don't always say the right thing, the right way, but as soon as I recognize I am behaving badly because my words are not coming out the way they should, I apologize. And then I realize I am here again. That I am having a hard time in this place. And then I let myself feel, so I can deal, in order to heal.

Tonight, I am wrapping presents. I am staying in the spirit, and it feels good. To be happy is my choice. I swear I can hear my sisters telling me, "Yes, use that wrapping paper. Not that bow, the other one!" It kinda trips me out. But I also like to hear them…. I know my family is with me and wouldn't leave me here alone. I know they are with me helping me make decisions, guiding me in my process. It's hard, but knowing they are on my shoulders makes it a little better…even though it's unbearable at times. They take some of my pain away by leaving glitter all over the place at Christmastime.

As usual, my tears have cleared my vision again. And now all I can hear are raindrops after a long drought. I feel I am about to rise from the ashes. The thought came to me yesterday, and now it's all I can think about. The prospect of a new year being right around the corner makes me think 2015 is the year to come into my own, with the help of my family.

99

Equation

Tonight, I had drinks with a friend who was not as close as I thought. When I was taking out my anger and angst over my family dying on her and another friend or two, thinking they would understand and come out of the smoke clearing as my friend, they actually were not my close friends. I am okay with it, and I did figure out along the way that they were not so close. That was my unfortunate finding because I feel truly bad they got the brunt of my dark heart.

I cannot act like what I handed them or any of my friends was pleasant. It was downright difficult and ugly. I was ugly on the inside and could not just get counseling. I was so raw and fucked up inside my head and soul and very being. I was so fucked each and every time my family members would die that I didn't have any idea how I was affected. I didn't know until I was in the situation and behaving badly.

I also could have no idea I would behave that way. I feel bad. I really don't feel like I should be forgiven. I am okay with that. I was simply where I was in that most fucked up time in my life. I feel so badly about how I affected my friends. I feel like I need to move away from them and make connections with new friends. I don't want to see the way they look at me and walk on eggshells. I really don't want to affect people in that way. It truly upsets me. I wonder if maybe I don't want to be around these friends because I behaved badly and am embarrassed, or because we just don't connect. I guess time will tell.

I am the only one I have to look to right now...and I am not about to think it was everyone else. Oh no, I don't do that. I only have myself to look to, and it's a lot to look at, even when I am in a positive light. Maybe I keep thinking I want to move away because I want to get away from myself. Hmm.... But I will still be there. What a fucked-up thing to realize about oneself. But, oh, so necessary! It's not them. It's me. What a rude awakening. I am so humble in this moment.

When you go through some really heavy shit and people don't behave the way you think they should, it's easy to give them up. Right now, I find I am the one who should be given up on. And I am so very disappointed in myself. I only went to the place in my hurt and my pain, and I don't really remember thinking about how anyone else was feeling. Unless their pain or situation was worse than mine, I disregarded and dismissed it. Oh, boy. It seemed easy to do while I was experiencing it. Now, I can clearly see how unattractive I was to be around. I didn't like myself during it all. I didn't even want to live my own life. I would have gladly traded it all. Unfortunately, that's not possible, and it gives me great perspective on how to have compassion for the pain others are going through, even though I may not understand it. Giving unconditional love when I don't think someone deserves it because they have lashed out at me. Forgiving when I feel I don't deserve the unkind words I was given. This is really hard stuff to do. But it is possible when you take yourself out of the equation.

100

Losing David Bowie

Losing David Bowie was more than just losing an amazing artist. Somehow, it was a personal loss. It was losing memories of my sister getting ready to go out on dates when I was just a kid. It was my very first concert in high school. It was losing a man who truly understood what it meant to reinvent himself.

I just watched a documentary on David. I never really understood his impact during his lifetime. He thought it, and then did it. He collaborated. He knew instinctively whom to work with in the music industry. And I had no idea of that in 1983 when I saw him in his Let's Dance tour at the Angel Stadium in Anaheim, California. He was thirty-six, and I thought he was a hot old man! At the time, I thought he was a cool old guy. Well, I have news for you young whippersnappers. What I'd give to go back to thirty-six. He was in his prime. I'm now forty-eight. You never really understand where you are when you are there—not until you wish you could go back. Which really sucks because you can't. Well, I am here to tell anyone younger than me, "Live each and every moment you have to live." If it's travel, do it. If it's love, find it. If it's career, build it. If it's laying around and wishing, you better get up now. Life will pass you by, and you better believe you have complete and utter control over each and every moment that passes you by.

My sisters died at forty-nine and fifty. That is not a full life. I just broke down in full sobbing tears because every time I think about how young they were when they first got sick, I realize just how lucky I am in my lifetime. Karen was twenty-nine when she got leukemia. Gayle was thirty-four when she got her brain tumor. One fought for her life. The other never knew what hit her. Both lives were debilitated. Both families were never the same. One husband killed himself. One young man started his family. One husband took care of his wife until the day she died. One woman's heart turned dark, but then found light from her new baby. It is all a choice. We all get to choose our attitude. We get to change our minds. We get to choose a direction. We may not get to choose when our life ends, but in the meantime, we get an awful lot of choices. Just waking up and choosing to be happy or to feel gratitude is an amazing feeling. And each and every day of our lives, we live with that choice. No matter what the circumstances are on any given day. We still get to choose our attitudes. We get to choose.

I don't know if you noticed, but David Bowie pretty much worked until he died. He lived until sixty-nine and smoked throughout his adult life. That's fine. It was his choice. And I kinda think we go when we are supposed to go. But he chose to reinvent himself every step of the way. He decided to shift when he knew he was in over his head, whether it was drugs or stagnation. His song "Heroes" says it all for me. Why not get up tomorrow with the attitude of being a hero? What a profound statement. We all know about the ripple effect. It can start a spectacular chain reaction, so let's do it. Let's be the change. I am putting my innermost self out there, and it is intense, but I do it anyway. What can you do to put your innermost self out there? And what kind of difference do you think it can make?

What will you choose? All I can think about is this: How can I make a change in one person's life tomorrow…or today?

101

Marathing

Lately, I've been noticing my journey. Not what I've been through, but where I am now. And most importantly, where I'm going. The present is all we have. Our health is all we really have. And if we are to live for now, well then, we gotta have both going on. Deep breath. I was just noticing what I am deeming as important in my life. I just ran another half-marathing—I just inadvertently typed that and found it very amusing. I think I will have to call them that from now on.

A marathing! I'm going to run a marathing. Ha! Maybe not, but after I ran the last one, all I could think while training was, *This is boring and I am running my last half-marathon.* The minute I got home, I saw a Facebook post of a three-year-old child who has had leukemia for half of his life, and from the photos I saw, he is struggling. He broke my heart all over again. He has "moon face" from the drugs, a feeding tube coming out of his nose, and most of all, the fighting spirit! I can see it. I can see it when he hugs his sister from her neck up. I can see he wants to play again and be a little boy. But this shitty thing that is making his life so difficult is stopping him from doing the things he really wants to do. This thing is called cancer. And he is looking tired.

I've been done with it. I won't look at it. I won't listen to it. I won't give it life. I refuse. I refuse to acknowledge its very existence. Yes that's right, I refuse! I won't get it because I refuse. This fucking thing is cancer.

But then I see this little boy, and I realize he never knew what hit him.

He didn't even know cancer existed. Before he knew it, it had consumed him and his young family. And now I must do something. All over again. I must run, maybe swim, maybe bike, and most definitely fundraise! It is the only thing I can do to feel like I can inspire something greater than myself. I have balanced out my own life by living it and making sure I have lived. But now I see it isn't all about me. It's about humanity. And even though I will live a long, full life, this little boy may not. So, I am here to stand up and do whatever I can to help. It may only do a little for the greater good, but I can't help but think it will inspire hearts, souls, and minds. That is a profound accomplishment in this day and age.

So my journey continues. Not from where I left off making sure I am having fun and fulfilling my happiness, but from this other place of wanting to help humanity in a profound way. I know I am only here for a short while, but while I am here for that blip, I will do my best to make that blip shine ever so brightly! That is the very reason for my heart to go on. Life is like a merry-go-round, ever-changing, and sometimes it goes up, and sometimes it goes down. When it goes down is when you gotta jump on and help in any way you can—any way possible. Help people less fortunate than you. Think about it—someone who is less fortunate than yourself. They may be homeless, hungry, or have cancer. We are so fortunate, but we seem to forget that because we get so caught up in our everyday lives. Everyday life gets mundane and trivial. Do something inspiring. I guarantee it will cause a ripple effect. And life will regain a beauty we have never seen before.

102

Gonna Be Special

I'm trying to work tonight, but I can't see through my tears. Leo, my prom date from high school, died and I am beside myself. I had no idea his death would affect me this way. I am truly feeling a loss, and I know why. I have been playing the music he shared with me. He first showed me his panache and style with Patti Austin's song "It's Gonna Be Special," and I loved it all! When Pat sent me over a photo of us in high school tonight, I lost it. I fell apart. We remained friends over the years. He came to visit me in Santa Barbara and he and my friend Henrietta hit it off in a very big way! And the two of them made me feel like the parent on that visit.

Leo was gay, and back in 1985, I fell in love with him. (Of course, I didn't know he was gay then). But I remember the moment. We went to dinner. He was driving me in his green 1960s Mustang, and when he put on his glasses to see, there was this moment for me. I fell in love.

It didn't last because Leo was gay, but we were friends from then on. When he got sober, he invited me to the ceremony in L.A. I went to support him, love on him, and be honest with him. I am pretty sure he is one of my soul mates, and I will miss him for the rest of my life. I took it for granted that I could call him, see him on Facebook, or get in touch with him. A very high price to pay when I can't contact my friend anymore. I will admit some of his choices made me stay away at times, but nonetheless, I would be there if he needed me, when he was being honest with me. I know, it sounds like a rule, but I needed it.

Last year, we celebrated our thirty-year high school reunion, and all I could think was that no time had passed. But it has. I now know what losing my family is like, but losing this friend is also a pretty awesome loss. Leo and I weren't close the last few years, but that doesn't change how I feel about him. We all go through difficult times and lose our way. At our reunion, I felt something was off with him, but I knew he would be back around and I would see my friend again. I was wrong. Time ran out to do so, and now I am at a loss. I can only hope he will visit me in my dreams. I have learned that is how our loved ones on the other side can visit us. So, I will look forward to our time together even if only in my sleep. I have learned to be content with this now and am thrilled when my family comes to see me. I'll be thrilled when Leo visits me too, even if he's dressed like he was on Halloween 1985 as the devil and his black-lip-liner turned my lips and face black when he kissed me. I was so content at that moment.

103

Heavy Heart

I had lunch with my ex-boyfriend Joe today. I reached out to him, and he agreed to meet me. I had a gift certificate and wanted to take him to lunch. He has a new girlfriend now, so it wasn't romantic, just as friends.

After lunch, I received a text from him that said, "Sorry I had to run off so quick. I'm sad now for some reason. You are one of the best people I know, and any guy would be lucky to have you in their life."

I am not in a relationship right now, but I am ready to be in love. It took me almost three years to feel like I am ready for love after all the loss, grief, and sadness. And nothing could make me happier than knowing I am in a place to feel love again. I wasn't sure I would ever feel like this again when I was in grief mode, but today, I am here to say that my heavy heart has lightened and the blackness has cleared away.

104

May

May will always be an interesting month for me now. I will never forget it is the month I watched my sister Karen die. I never wanted to say it changed me, but it has. I no longer look at life the same way. It's true, but not in the ways you would think. I no longer think of May as the month before summer starts, but as the month life ended for Karen and changed for me. I think about that time when I had to do the things I didn't want to do, but I did them with all the love in my heart to make my sister feel comfortable in the last days of her life. I knew I would never have the chance again. Ever.

I am now at the age my sisters were when they both died. I am in a numb state of mind. I don't know how I feel about it all, but I know something is brewing inside of me right now. It's like all of the moments when I couldn't feel anything but angst, only now I can identify the feeling of inner turmoil. I guess that's what I will call it today.

So, I am turning an age that I don't like at all. Forty-nine sounds old to me, and I don't like it. I see my skin changing among other things I do not wish to discuss, and that's so not like me at all. I love talking about all the things nobody told me would happen to my body. But I see the changes of an aging person and don't like it. I see my youth behind me. I see things on my body shifting and doing things I don't really care for. All I want to do is commiserate with my mom and sisters about their experiences. But I can't, and it is pissing me off. Damn it! I want to talk about it with them, and laugh about it, and make it a joke, and get over it.

The other thing I lack is a man. I really want love in my life again. And that is so exciting to me. Because at a certain point, I never thought my heart would heal. I am here to tell you it has done a lot of healing. It will never stop, I am told. And as ready as I feel, it is a slow process. So, I trust. I trust I am where I am supposed to be—again. And as soon as I remember, I relax.

Last weekend, I took care of my childhood friend who has MS. That fucking sucks. She is almost completely debilitated. She can no longer move her body. She can *not* move her body. Completely unable. And as much as it makes me sad, it inspires me. Her mental attitude and drive are the most inspirational acts any human can have. She can no longer move her body, and yet her spirit soars!

So, back to May. It was the month Karen gave up—but not until the very end. She no longer wanted to fight. And I could not blame her. She was fucking dying and so miserable. Her pain was horrible, and if she hadn't been on the morphine pain pump, I think the pain would have killed her. It only took five days for her spirit to leave once she told me she didn't want to *do this* anymore. I wish I could say it was a relief. But it wasn't. It was the first day of the rest of my life without my sister—my sister, my confidant, my friend who knew me better than anyone. Karen and I became so close when Gayle got brain cancer and was never the same again after her surgery. We shared the kind of sister stuff without ever speaking a word of it. We didn't have to; we knew each other to the soul. We were sisters.

So the changes in me are clear at least for now:

1. **Laugh at everything remotely funny.** Okay, I already do that, but it didn't happen for a very long time when they were all dying.

2. **Live the life I am here to live.** Don't let the pain of my past stop me from my journey.

3. **Look for the silver lining in every cloud.** Life is fragile and can be over at any moment. And that is okay too. We only get this time while we are here, and I think we are here to learn lessons—lessons we missed in other lifetimes or we just can't seem to master.

4. **Cry.** Whenever something is sad, happy, or just frustrating as all hell!

5. **Be fearless.** What do I have to fear now? My greatest fear was my family dying. They're dead. I am still living, and I am here to tell you I have a journey and it's mine. It includes all the loss, heartache, tears, and grief. But it also includes strength, healing, grieving, getting back up, gratitude, love, fun, writing this book, and so much more.

6. **I'm going to start checking things off my bucket list.** Prince was on my bucket list, but now I can never see him in concert. I was

pretty bent outta shape from his loss. And it made me understand that putting things off and never getting around to them is a bad idea. So, now it is time for me to start checking things off of my bucket list.

7. **I *must* see the Aurora Borealis in this lifetime.** So, now that I am at the age when my sisters died, I am planning my trip. I know they will be there with me. I already felt them when I went to the travel agent. Their excitement was greater than mine! I started crying and couldn't stop it. I do not like public crying, but there it was. And I just apologized and explained my situation because it makes people uncomfortable.

8. **Make plans.** Now that I've been bit by the travel bug, I find it important to have things to look forward to. Places to go, people to see, and things to do. Even if it's simply spending time with my friends. Plan it, or it may not happen.

9. **Keep pushing myself.** Why lay down and let my hopes die too? There was a time when I didn't think I could live without my family. It was a hard time when I felt hopeless, but I am not there anymore.

10. **Live now.** Live now. *Live now!* It is a present tense state of mind. I can't live now, tomorrow. Or yesterday. Or any other day. I can only live now! Especially since I am feeling like my youth is behind me. Who fucking cares? Don't stop 'til it's over. This is my new mantra: If I am alive, it's not over. I will keep reminding myself until the day I die. Keep living now. Won't stop 'til it's over.

I feel like I am rambling, but all I am really trying to say is that my heart is full. I am happy, and this is the youngest I will be from today on…

so I may as well feel young today. All I know is that it's a trip when they leave, and I am just making it up as I go.

Yesterday was the seven-year anniversary of Karen leaving this planet. My day was nice. But at one point I came to a stoplight and there was a man in a wheelchair. His spine was so bent, and he looked like he had been through a war. My heart sank. I looked around my car and found half of my sandwich from lunch. I rolled my window down and asked if he was hungry. He replied, "I'm always hungry!" Then he started telling me things, and he was so joyful and full of life. It broke my heart, and I drove away crying. In that moment, I knew my life was so great. Yep. My head is down, letting my vision clear again. Crying always help me see so clearly after.

105

Holiday Tunnel

It's that time of year again. Just when I think I am okay and have come to a new place in my healing journey, the holidays come and take me back ten steps. The music in the stores still kills me and almost brings me to tears every single time. I usually have things to look forward to and places to go, but not this year. I am here to just look it in the face and deal with it on my own. No one can really help me. It's all mine. This year I do feel a little alone. I'm so glad my plan of having no children is working out so well right now. Oh, God, I hate this place, but I know if I don't get it out of me, it will stay inside of me, and so here I am again writing.

I feel the heaviness in my heart, and there is not much I can do to alleviate it except cry. Crying always seems to help get it out. Watching a sad movie or playing some songs that take me to another place are always good too. But writing about it and getting it out is my therapy. It's only the beginning of the holiday season, and I am wanting to put up a Christmas tree for the first time in three years. There is that sadness that doesn't want anything to do with it. But today, I bought a tree stand, so it's a good sign.

I just keep wanting to surround myself with my favorite people who make me feel like family and whom I love. I will do that as soon as I can. Although the last time I felt this way, my friends were concerned. Thankfully, the holidays keep me busy. I will plan my trips as soon as I can to solace my heart and soul. I completely understand at this point in my healing journey how important that is for my survival.

I still can't believe I have days when all I want to do is call my sisters. I get the thought out of my mind as quickly as possible to avoid any additional heart-fucking pain. I have been feeling good for so long now. I didn't see this one coming. Maybe it comes when I have not felt for too long. Even though I felt like I was out of the dark tunnel, I guess there will always be more tunnels to get through. It's a never-ending process. I guess I will call this my "Holiday Tunnel," and it comes when it wants. Without warning.

I found myself coaching myself today, "Just keep your mouth shut. Don't drag innocent bystanders into your turmoil." That's not fair. I had a good day of not dragging others into my shit. Sometimes I just cry and get out what I have to get out that day. And that's a good day.

Understanding the angst inside you is so important. Listen to it when you feel sad. Heartache. Inexplicable pain. If you give it some attention, you will find where it's coming from. And then you can give it some love—self-love—and understand that it's okay to feel. And deal. So you can heal. Even though you thought you were past this point in your healing.

106

Giver

I am feeling euphoric in my heart right now, and I don't know why. I just keep having this sensation to cry because I am happy. Happy in my life. Not one life experience can erase, take away, or change the wonderful feeling I am having in this moment.

This year has been extraordinary. I bought my first home and everything just fell into place. I did not know that was what this year would bring, but I do now. It is Christmastime and the holidays are *so* very hard because it's so easy to remember the past. My mom and her perfect lights on the tree, cooking every meal with such love. All the excitement Christmas brought when I was younger. This year, I decorated the tree of my friend Sam, who also has MS and can no longer walk. I wanted to, and I made it perfect, just like my mom would have liked. I even did eighties high-impact aerobics to be entertaining, although I think I laughed harder than anyone! I participated in our holiday parade, even though I did not dance. I should have. I should have been out there with everyone having fun. I had fun blowing the bubble machine, but

I should have been dancing in this thing called life. Another night, I dressed up, went on a pub crawl with a bunch of people, and had a great time. Again, dancing was in order. I love to dance freely. It makes me feel happy. Even though there was a glitch and my family will not all be together, I am embracing those in my family who do want to be a part of the holidays. And we are creating new traditions like a "nice" gift elephant exchange. And game playing this year. And no one cooks. Unless they really want to, of course.

Even though I think I am ready for love, I have not found it in a man just yet. I am now in the place to recognize that it is time to give thanks for the people in my life who were there to support me when my family was dying. This is pretty huge, even though I have known the entire time who it was all along. Joe made a huge impact in my life, but when we were together, I had no idea. It's amazing what we can learn once we are no longer in the thick of things. When I was with Joe, I always wanted to run, but I never knew why. That was so unlike me. He was there for me, and now I want to appreciate him. I took him some yummy treats today and said, "Thank you for being my support system for the worst three years of my life." We will always be friends. I had no idea when I was in that moment, but I do now. And I am feeling so grateful.

Tonight, I looked across the way to my neighbors' houses and saw the lights of their Christmas trees and teared up again. Earlier today, I was looking in my closet at a jacket my sister gave me. It is a little too small. I haven't been able to part with it because she gave it to me, but lately, I have been finding myself in a place of giving. I am warm in my new home, while some people have no place to go tonight and are cold. I keep thinking my sister is telling me to let it go so it can warm someone up this winter. And I am ready…and I am tearing up again. It's not easy to let their things go, even after six-and-a-half years. But I know it's time because it's now bugging me to leave.

Dying is a sure end to life, but I am convinced the other side is where all the magic happens. It's only those of us left behind who suffer. And that's okay. Today, while I was shopping for my great-niece, I saw a sign that said, "Even when we go, we are still with you…." That's a sure sign they are just saying "Hi" and they are always with me.

107

Instead

It's been more than four years since my life has calmed down to a normalcy. So much healing has taken place in my heart, in my soul, and in my tears. My tears have subsided a lot. They can come when I summon them, but I don't do that needlessly. I do it when I need to cry and feel. I do it when I miss my family. I do it when something so overwhelming makes me think of them that I cannot hold back. I do it when I dream of them. That one always makes me cry. I wake up and realize it was a dream. And it breaks my heart all over again.

I have found a new normalcy. For this, I am eternally grateful. I am on my new path, which seems very familiar. I love what I do, and I have help along the way. I no longer feel like I am in this alone. For that, I am grateful. Life really does go on—if you let it. If you let the initial heartbreak take you down, it will truly take you down. Even if you don't let it take you down, there will be stuff dragging you into the abyss. It's a very dark and sad place to go. Try to avoid it, and guess what? You will still go to a very sad and dark place. It's inevitable. It's unavoidable. And you have no choice. So just go. But know this. You will come back. It is a choice. And you have to choose it. Life will keep happening in a much nicer fashion, so keep your head up and just keep moving forward. Surround yourself with friends who feel like family. They will take you in and make you feel protected. At least that is what I have found.

I find that I don't write as much anymore. What needed to get out is much less intense, and I am so glad for this. I am in the light now. Before, it was a light at the end of a tunnel, and I know that's a cliché, but I find that those stupid clichés got me through a lot. Listen to them. They weren't written without a lesson, a reason, or a way to understand a situation. One of my favorites is still "God doesn't give you more than you can handle." And I am not a religious person. But in my journey, I have found more belief in God than in my religious upbringing. I know it sounds like I had belief from my religious upbringing, but I didn't. It truly came from my journey. And as painful and heartbreaking as it has been, I would not trade it for anyone else's life.

Back to my healing heart and my life moving on. I am really feeling like I am ready for love again. It's been a long time—ten years. I miss it. I have a longing to feel it again. I have been single for four years now, and I can only figure that there is something I am meant to do right now instead.

108

Watch

Lately, I feel it is time to focus on my career. All I can hear in my head is, "If you ever wanna make God laugh, make a plan." I have hired a business coach, an awesome assistant, and an intern, and still, things are about the same. I have been working hard at shutting up my defensive, defeated inner voice, but today I was putting away photo albums from the 1990s and found myself crying and sharing the photos with my nephews and niece who have never even seen these photos of their moms before. They were my memories. Now they can remember too.

No matter how hard I try to make myself do the things I know I should to grow my business, I don't. I can't even figure myself out. I want it. I have had great business success in the past. I've thrived! But right now, I am stagnating.

I do feel a little like my life is slipping by. My youth is behind me, and it is really making me sad. I really want to talk to my mom and sisters, but I can't. I really don't know how I am feeling right now. I am right at the age when my sisters died. I am forty-nine and turning fifty this year. Karen died at forty-nine and Gayle at fifty. I am right there. I don't think that it is affecting me until I find myself in a funk—a funk I have never known. I haven't been here before, but now I'm here. I felt I wouldn't want to live a long life without my family, but I have found a new stride and am feeling like I am thriving again. But I am having a hard time figuring out what is stopping me with this business thing. Why don't I just get over myself, make calls, and do the things I know will move me forward? I can't keep using my past as my excuse. I don't believe in that.

All of a sudden, it occurred to me. What if my angels are leading me right to where I am supposed to be? I'm turning fifty in six months, and the shock of my youth being behind me is softening. I am now realizing that I haven't seen anything! I know I *have* to see the Aurora Borealis in my lifetime, so for my fiftieth, I am now in hot pursuit of it. Now that I know what I need to do, my path seems clear. And yes, I do feel a little calmer in my soul—as if my family knows and is encouraging me.

Today, I was cleaning, going through boxes, and clearing a place for something new. I came across a watch. It was my mom's and so delicate and sweet. It is white gold with tiny little diamonds and inscribed from 1956 "Love, Mother and Dad." Now I am wearing it. I thought to look at the time on it and it was 12:03. At first, I didn't think much of it, but then it occurred to me that my clock in my bathroom has been stopped at 12:03 for a while now. Wow. What a coincidence, or is it? I truly felt it was my mom saying, "Hi." Whoa.... When I put the watch on, the time didn't move, but now after an hour or so, it is at 12:15. Time has started moving again. Maybe it's a reminder that I, too, am not here forever, and now is the time to live my life.

I just looked again at the time, and it is now 12:23, and it's so small that my almost-fifty eyes can't frickin' see it, and that's making me mad all over again! I know. I know. I wish they were here to say it to me in person. It's hard getting old without them.

109

Community

Santa Barbara is broken right now. In December and January, we experienced the largest fire in California's history. It was the worst disaster I've seen in my twenty-nine years living here. The fire wasn't even officially out when the most torrential downpour of rain came during the night. A half-inch came down in five minutes, on a freshly burned hillside. I've heard that a half-inch in an hour can inspire a mudslide. No one could have predicted what would happen. The weatherman said, "It's gonna rain, and it's gonna rain hard!" The sheriff went door to door for hours telling residents to evacuate. A lot did not. They had evacuation fatigue from the fire. What happened next was unspeakable. It brings tears to my eyes every time I think of the loss of lives, homes, and a beautiful little community.

I woke up at 6:30 a.m. and immediately turned on the news because I knew something had probably happened in the night because of the rain they predicted. What I saw was devastating. It was still dark, so they couldn't really see all that had been destroyed. Initially, three homes were completely gone from their slabs. Then daylight came and true devastation was revealed. The mud/ash and water had come down that hillside with such a fury and vengeance that hell would have been scared. Boulders the size of cars moved like pebbles. The streets were littered with them! Homes were splintered into toothpicks, smashed into neighbors' yards, and people were found dead in the streets. I couldn't believe it when I saw on the news that a body had washed down Olive Mill Road right by The Biltmore. My friend Connie lives right there. That human flowed right passed her house! Later, I heard that cars, debris, and maybe bodies made it to the ocean and were washed out to sea. I was horrified and glued to the news the entire day. I could not believe the devastation of Montecito. My heart was breaking for the families and their loved ones who had yet to discover what a devastating blow this was about to become for them. Homes can be built, things can be replaced, but our loved ones will be missed forever. So far, nineteen lives will be missed with the most heart-wrenching sadness that some may ever feel from knowing their loved ones died in the Montecito debris flow. There are no words that will ever help them through this pain and heartache. For this, I am so very sorry.

One thing I sense so strongly in Santa Barbara and all its adjoining cities is our community. As a community, we look after each other. We care. We support each other's kids, causes, and businesses. We know each other's kids, schools, and where we like to shop because we are a community. We started small, and now we are growing, so it's our job to teach the new residents how we do it here. New folks are moving here because they fell in love with our community; they fell in love with all the wonderful things we are. That's why I fell in love and never left after college. Yet they bring their own ideas and energy, which affects the very community they fell in love with. Now, why would you want to disrupt this community by bringing a different energy into it?

We have experienced a lot of natural disasters in Santa Barbara. Fires and floods, but not to this degree. No one could have seen this catastrophic disaster coming because it has never happened before. This event was unprecedented, and no one could have predicted its magnitude! Yet people want to blame and ask why it happened. Why weren't there any alarms? Really? In Montecito? Isn't that why you live there—because it's low key and there are no alarms? Oh, and this has *never* happened before. But I get it; when you are a victim to the most horrific event that has ever hit your community, you want answers! Unfortunately, God is the only one with answers. This was of biblical proportion, at least for this community. At best, we can learn from it, put plans into place, and hope it never happens again. I have a feeling it won't.

One reason we all love living here is because we are resilient, forgiving, and know how to move on without taking this lovely little city down. The national news just wants to sensationalize like always. I saw that during the Thomas Fire. I was disenchanted and remembered why I only watch our local news. I heard a local celebrity talking to her fans on a tour of her home in Montecito soon after the mudslide. I wondered how she got on her property? By helicopter? I don't know, but her big news was the fence she lost and some gardens. I thought, *WTF? People died and their homes were disintegrated! You lost a fence.* I couldn't believe what I was hearing. But I get that she was experiencing the mudslide in her own way.

There are so many things we all can do to make our town great. Our community is special, so let's keep it that way. Victim or survivor—which are you? Victorious, I hope.

So, if you are new to this community, perhaps from a big city, know that we won't adhere to your new ideas, but you will adopt our resilient and special energy.

110

Forgiveness Is Love

I'm not sure I'm prepared to write this chapter, but I believe it's important because of all the revelations I've had. So here it goes.... I met a guy I really liked from the beginning, but he didn't seem available. We met online, and the first night we messaged, we discovered both of our dads flew for Delta and probably knew each other. They both flew out of LAX and retired within two years of each other. Back then, it was about good ole boys, and they all knew each other.

I couldn't decipher whether this guy was physically or emotionally unavailable. He is also a pilot and works a lot. We met online on the three-year anniversary of my dad's death, and his dad had passed only four months earlier. When we met in person, I liked him—always a bad sign. I think he liked me too based on the text he sent me only minutes after we parted ways that night. But then I didn't hear from him for a week or so. It went on and on like this for a year. He would let me know he was working a lot. And because I really liked him, I would understand and have patience. But then I'd had enough. He texted me one night to ask what I was doing. I replied, "Ignoring you." I told him I was looking for something that only slightly resembled a relationship. I was cutting him off. He proceeded to text me. I kept putting him off, which seemed to make him only want me more. I admit, I was weak at times. It was hard to deny him when I really liked him. My heart started feeling, which made it a bad situation for me. I kept looking for something new, but it never came. Ugh. I was really trying to move to love and I couldn't find it, but he would not relent. I would tell myself I still needed sex until I found someone. And I would always know it was because I felt something in my heart for this man. That's why I had to cut him off. Or at least try.

Fast forward another year. One night, he contacted me when I was at my friend's house, only one mile away from where he was. Yep, you guessed it. I went. And it was awesome! The best time I believe we ever had. Heavy sigh.... This is still really fresh, and it's still hard for me. I am still processing it. I have feelings for this human. My heart wanted what it wanted. So the next part is so full of mixed emotions. Two days after I saw him, I decided to type in his name on social media. What I found was exactly what every woman never wants to see. Photos of him and another woman in many scenarios. The scenarios I wished to be in! She was living the life I hoped to live with him. My heart dropped, but it all made sense in that second. I sent him a scathing text, letting him know I was on to him. He called me immediately, most likely so I wouldn't send a message to his "on and off again" girlfriend. I made sure to say everything I needed to say so I wouldn't regret it later. We hung up when there was nothing left to say.

The next day, I remembered he was the age my dad was when he told me he had a mid-life crisis, so I thought I would let him know it was something most humans go through. I couldn't help caring about this man. Ugh. I don't know if I am fucked up or if it's just this thing called life or this guy I call Don Key. Oh boy, you should see the slew of texts I sent him, things like "How do you fuck with other humans' emotions like that?" I felt pretty scorned. But wait. There's more.... He was really sick, throwing up and not feeling good at all that day. I told him,

"Karma is working fast!" He said he couldn't partake in his shaming because he was so ill. I replied, "I am not shaming you. I am surprised that is even possible considering the narcissistic, heartless, shell of a human you are. I just wanted you to know your actions have an effect on other people who do have hearts, and I will never understand how you can hurt others like you do. I just don't get it."

The next day, he replied, "Good morning. That's an interesting idea. I've been fucked up since my dad died over two years ago now." Oh, fuck! I figured he had gone through his grief by now. I was wrong. What transpires next was such a massive and compassionate understanding. I don't even know what else to call it. As it unfolded, I relived so much of my own stuff. I replied that maybe his dad's death was something he had not dealt with. "Grief is an interesting journey. It gets better, just so you know. It really fucked me up too, over and over and over and over. And I did the same thing as you did to my ex more than once. I cheated when they were all dying. This was a huge moment for me. I forgot all about that, and I realize I am no better than you, and *this* is probably *my* karma catching up to me. Hopefully, it wipes my karma slate clean and I get to find love and fun now."

I was so hugely in a moment in my own life that seeing exactly where he was in his shook me to my core. He shared with me that after he reflected on his actions, he couldn't figure out where and when he became fucked up. He had been more fucked up than he realized since his dad had passed. I understood. I told him, "Grief is quite a ride. It really does fuck you up, and you just don't care. If you don't deal and feel, you will have a harder time with your healing. This I know for a fact. And it sucks to feel it, but it will help you break through to the other side."

I believe something wonderful is still waiting to happen for me. I hope it's love that happens, but with whom I don't know. I still have feelings for this man. But for now we are friends. I have been sending him chapters of this book and he says it's helping. In fact, he said, "Bunny, publish your book!" Right now, I have not really done anything with it except blog it. I now have a fire burning under my book because I know it has helped one person with grief they didn't know how to move on from. Knowing I actually helped one person is huge. It is the only reason I am putting my own life story out there.

I'm sure you are wondering how I forgave him so fast. It wasn't a difficult decision. When my family died, it was so final. That's it! Gone! I can never carry on a conversation with any of them again. But this man is alive and I can carry on a friendship with him, so I chose to be friends because he is in my life and in my heart, and I don't want to lose another person. I would rather be friends than act like he was dead. It's a softer landing that way. Dead is so final, and I don't have to say goodbye forever, which is really hard to do, so I chose not to. It took me two days to forgive, and it felt a lot better than being mad at him and feeling scorned. My heart is still sad that things turned out this way, but I'm hopeful because I actually felt love again. He will always have a place in my life, and oddly, against my better judgment, I wish it was as my lover, confidant, and best friend. All because my heart wanted what it wanted.

111

Deep Breathing

Wow! I almost forgot that my dad died five years ago today. I suppose that's a good thing, a huge part of my moving forward, and I am so grateful for it. But I like to remember. I will never forget that phone call at 4 a.m. I was sleeping so hard that I didn't hear my phone ringing. Joe shook me awake. When I answered, it was the HB Police Department regretfully informing me that my father had passed away. All I kept saying was "What?" I was so confused and couldn't understand why.

It still hurts to know what a horrible human being the caregiver is. She had just watched us bury both of our sisters, mom, aunt, and now our dad. What kind of person can now steal some of the only things left from our family? I don't know and never will, but I do ask myself, "What lesson can I learn from this?" I came up with, "I gotta let it go." To hold on to those possessions will only take me down a path of negativity and resentment. A life I do not want to lead. Heavy and deep breath…and to continue from here on out. If this is the only thing I take from my family dying, that's just ridiculous. I have some of the best, worst, and most beautiful memories! And they are all bringing tears to my eyes.

112

Pillow Fluffer

"Can you fluff my pillow? Can you get me something to eat? Can you spread my fingers out? Can you move my shoulders toward you? Can you put the straw in my mouth? Can you move my legs?"

Does this sound like a demanding diva? It's not. It's my childhood friend finding her way through MS. She is a master at communicating her needs. She can no longer move her legs or right arm. Her left arm is starting to lose its movement too. Most of her has atrophied now. She has a bladder bag now. I'm not sure how much time she has left on this planet, but I marvel at her positive attitude, her will to live, and her strength to continue to raise her teenage son and twenty-two-year-old daughter—all from her bed and although they are already raised. Now they are in for the real deal. This is likely the last part of their journeys with their mom. The next part will be without her. It's a part I am not prepared to deal with.

Ari and I grew up three doors from each other, and we were buddies. Her family took me skiing and on trips to the Redwoods and their family cabin on June Lake. She and I used to sing songs into a tape recorder while wearing headphones. We couldn't hear what we sounded like when we sang, but we laughed our asses off when we heard the recording. We were like "peas and carrots" until high school. Then, we went off into our own worlds and hardly saw each other since I was a year older than her. We reconnected my senior year and had a little fun at a party.

We went on with our lives, getting married, she had kids, and life was moving along. I can't remember when I learned that she was diagnosed with MS. I didn't see her much because I moved 130 miles north. I wanted to reconnect with her, but life was moving us in all kinds of directions, kind of like how the ocean swishes you around. My family was getting cancer, and then her dad, Willy, died of lung cancer. Willy was one of my other dads. I knew how close he and Ari were based on a conversation I had with him after her diagnosis. He told me a story about Ari and ended it with "She is my hero" and tears in his eyes.

We didn't really reconnect again until my dad died and the caregiver tried to steal his house. Ari and her amazing husband Brian stepped up and helped me from beginning to end of the month-long fight. Having my childhood friend help me through one of the most stressful times in my life reconnected us in the most profound way.

Fuck. This is a hard chapter to write while I am here taking care of my friend. I am staying with her for the weekend so her loving, caregiving, selfless husband can take the weekend off. He is up at the cabin in June Lake with Ari's brother and friends having a good ole time. At least that's what I hope he's doing. Last year when he went on this annual trip, he came back and confessed that he felt guilty the whole time he was away. "Now what fun is that?" I asked. When someone gives you the weekend off, you gotta take advantage of it and have the time of your life. Go live, Brian!

But then I got it. His life is Ari. He loves her so much. She is his life. He told me his story a while ago. He didn't care if he lived or died before he met her. He is not a big man, but men feared him because he was fearless. He would beat them up. And he didn't really care what happened to him. In fact, I think he may have wanted to die. But then he met Ari and fell in love. He never looked back. They got married and had two kids. And now his life is taking care of the woman he loves. Perhaps he loves her more than his own life. I feel pretty certain of it.

This weekend, I am here to take care of my friend in the most loving way—with my heart, and with compassion and humor. Sound familiar? It should; it's what I learned from taking care of my own family. I should explain, though, that Ari won't just let anyone take care of her. It's a very intimate and personal experience for her and everyone involved. I was actually surprised when she asked me to help the first time because we had skipped so many years. I am so happy we get to make up for lost time now. She is my family. Her family is my family. I am not sure I know what to say about making her daughter and son cry this weekend. Oddly enough, both conversations were about tattoos. One already got one, and the other is going to get one. One loves hers, and the other said he's been thinking about it for a couple of years now, and he's only sixteen. He wants to get the handicap symbol to honor his mom. I was thinking it could be more artistic and pretty, and that's when I made him cry. He wants what he wants. I completely understand. And I shut my mouth. After I vehemently apologized, of course. After all, it takes a village to raise humans.

It also takes a whole lot of love, compassion, inner strength, wine, more love, laughter, friends, understanding, no judgment, humor, more wine, and physical strength to take care of a friend who only wants to feel normal in her fucked-up, debilitating situation. That's where I step in. I only come with love, compassion, pillow fluffing, food getting, finger spreading, straw guiding, leg and hand moving, and as a friend with a smile and a happy, cheerful disposition so my friend can enjoy some of her last moments of life knowing she is loved and can laugh and feel loved. My only answer is "Yes! What do you need?" How could I do otherwise? My friend can no longer move her body! And yet she is positive and happy, and she finds joy in the little things.

113

Lee

I've been teaching fitness at the YMCA for twenty-nine years now. I taught there when I was in college, when I gave my bone marrow to my sister, and when each of my family members died. When I began finding subs all the time, the members realized something was amiss. I would let some know, little by little, what was happening. But never everything at once unless I knew the member well and knew they could handle my shit. Or maybe I needed support and love in that moment. I couldn't even handle what was happening at the time, and to speak about it only made it real. I wasn't ready for it all to be real.

When Karen was dying, I needed breaks from being in that moment and went home just to teach my class—just to feel normal for one night. I'm sure I was a hot mess, but I always felt like I had my poker face on and needed to escape what was happening in my life. My sister was dying. It will be eight years next month, and when I write, I still feel like it is happening now. I am crying and don't really know how I got through all the loss when it was happening.

Today, while teaching at the YMCA, one of my favorite members, Lee, showed up before my class. I hadn't seen her in a while. She is an adorable Asian woman who disappears from time to time to go to Asia, so I didn't think much of her absence. But today I saw her hair loss and handkerchief on her head. I know what that means. I know why she is visiting me. I really only want to know she is going to be okay. Instead, she tells me her breast cancer has spread to her lungs. I know what that means too. My eyes filled with tears, and my heart filled with compassion. She said something like, "I know how many of your family members died of cancer, and I just wanted you to know." I don't remember exactly what she said, but I knew she was saying goodbye, and it broke my heart but simultaneously filled it with love. This human, whom I don't know very well, came to tell me she had cancer and she wanted me to know. I am guessing she also felt my human compassion, or maybe she is an angel! I don't know. I did learn she is a professor and still teaching. Maybe Lee is my reminder to feel and deal in order to heal. That's how it feels tonight. She also told me to keep doing yoga. I will if you will, Lee. Keep living, Lee! My heart is sore over this one.

114

Without You

Yesterday was a bit emotional, so I knew today would be tricky. Today, it's been eight years since Karen died. I thought I was past these kinds of days, but I was wrong. My grieving continues.... I am taking care of myself today. I did yoga and will go for a cleansing walk later. Breathe in and out.... Breathing seems like something I wouldn't forget to do, but deep breathing is necessary today. I keep listening to Vance Joy's song "Who Am I?" It asks who am I without you? I can tell you, Karen, I never wanted to know. I will never forget how I felt when I got the call that you had passed.

Even though we knew you were dying in the worst way, I still had no idea how I would feel. I felt horrible. I thought there would be relief after six weeks of watching you die, which was heart and gut wrenching. You were nothing but skin and bones. The cancer won and you were done. I left for a couple of days to go home and work and teach my class. I needed a break and hospice was so good at teaching us it was okay to leave and take breaks. They told us if you wanted us there when you left, you would wait. You didn't. The call was so distressful. It was done. And there was no going back and changing anything! I couldn't tell you I loved you one more time. I could never laugh with you again. I could never cry with you again. I could never celebrate one more happy life event with you ever again. This was truly sobering.

I never said goodbye because it was a ridiculous thing to say. And I couldn't. That would mean you were leaving. I couldn't bear the thought or the reality. And hard as it was to watch you suffer so tremendously, it was even harder to accept you were gone forever. I was in a weird state of accepting. I wanted to throw up. My heart felt like it was going to stop beating, and I was almost unemotional and unable to understand the magnitude of losing you and Gayle. Because I now had to figure out how to make arrangements for your funeral. And I had to pull my shit together. When I got back to your house, the hospital bed in your living room was empty. I wasn't ready for how I would feel seeing that! I felt so unprepared, even though we had just buried our sister four months prior. Today, I keep thinking I want to see you, talk to you, hug you, and laugh with you, but I can't. The only thing I can do is write you a letter, so that is what I am going to do.

Hi Karen,

I can't believe it's been eight years since you passed away. A lot has happened. After you two left this planet, Mom followed you one year and five months later. I'm sure you know this because she is with you. That was a really hard day because I never knew you wouldn't be here to support me and teach me how to live without our mom. It was pretty fucked up to have to figure it out on my own. Oh, and that's when I became the matriarch of our family. That kind of tripped me out. I am not even a mother, and now I am the eldest woman in our family. What the hell! How did this happen?

After Mom passed away, Auntie died nine months later. That was a trip because it was just Bobby and me, and no one let us know how far along with Parkinson's she had gotten. I went to visit her a couple of months prior and could clearly see she was not well. We were her only family besides her friends, and it was up to Bobby and me to figure out the rest. Things went to probate and we are still dealing with it. It is a mess! Her will was outdated. She only named Mom, you, and Gayle as beneficiaries. Who would have thought she would outlive you all? It is true, people come out of the woodwork when they think they can get their hands on money. Thirteen Polish people who never even met Auntie are trying to take what they can. It is truly sad to see this, but since it is taking almost six years to decide the outcome, it has given me the opportunity to let it go. Our attorney is taking her second maternity leave—that's how long this is taking! It's a joke! Anyhow, after Auntie died, Dad was moving along. He went green—he put solar panels on the house, got a hybrid car, and was fixing up the house. He had some gumption left. He kept the caregiver after Mom passed to help him. He wasn't used to living alone and without a wife after fifty-two years of marriage. And now he was on his own again. He seemed to be embracing his newfound single life. He turned eighty, but less than three weeks later, he died too—only seven months after Auntie. The doctors said he had cancer and started treating him with chemo. I kept saying before his first treatment that the chemo would kill him. I was right, but I had no idea it would kill him the same night! What happened after that was human unkindness. The fucking caregiver tried to steal our house! Yes, the house we grew up in! It was so stressful and horrible, but we got through that too.

Once we got rid of the caregiver, Bobby and I had the lovely chore of clearing out our home of over fifty years. Heavy sigh. Fifty years of stuff! And you know what a collector of things Dad was. Oh, and thank you for saving all the lovely things you and Mom saved in the attic. Haha! That was fun going through all your stuff. I am kidding, but now I realize it was part of our healing. It was part of dealing with the loss of all of you. I never imagined life without you and Gayle. Never in a million years did I ever think I wouldn't have you by my side going through all the memories of our life. That part really sucked. Bobby took so much stuff home. It was part of his grief. He wasn't ready to let go. It's been five years since Dad died, and he is finally letting go of all the stuff he took home. Lari is relieved.

On a happier note, you both have beautiful grandchildren now. Karen, you died three months after Kayden was born. You wanted to live for her and your son Travis. And now he has another fun-spirited daughter named Hazel. Both girls have stolen my heart. And Erica has a fun little boy named Roan, who is pure joy. He is such a happy boy and I have so much fun competing with Grandpa Dan at Christmastime to buy his favorite present. I won last Christmas. They are all doing well and so is James. He is figuring out life and getting through his grief. After losing his mom and going through anger issues with his sister, he is doing quite well, and I am proud of him.

It's been five years since Dad died now. I have told the Universe there will be no more deaths in our family for thirty years. I refuse to plan another funeral or grieve another loss in my family. I wrote all four of your eulogies and stood up at the funerals to tell the world about my sisters and parents. I knew I would regret it if I didn't. It really sucked, and I cannot find another way to explain the loss I felt when you all left. My heart was black, but I kept on moving forward through it all, and I have figured out how to live again.

I am going to Italy in two weeks, and I am so excited. I have never been abroad. It wasn't really about me when you were all ill and going through your sicknesses, so I didn't go very far. But now I am making it about me and I am going to travel! My last birthday was difficult because I turned the age you both died at, so I knew I had to look forward to something. We went to Sedona for my birthday, and it was amazing. I'm going to Italy now, and to Norway in January to see the Northern Lights. I feel fairly certain I will cry when I see them. I know you all will be there with me too. The Northern Lights are the number-one thing on my bucket list, and I have to do it *now*. There is no time to wait. You have all taught me that. I can't wait any longer.

I wish I was doing this fun stuff with you, Gayle, and Mom. Even though I know you all will be with me, it's still pretty bittersweet. A whole lot of bitter with only a little sweet. But I must live on. I miss you all so much, but I try not to think about it too much because it's a lot. It's a lot to miss you so tremendously. I know you are all with me, but none of you talk back to me. I miss our banter, Karen, and listening to Dad yell at us and Mom always saying it goes in one ear and out the other. Those days are gone, and I am recreating my family with friends who are like family to me. No one can replace you, but I have to find the souls I connect with and can tell anything to. Just like I did with you.

My heart is healing, but for some reason, it was hurting today. I couldn't catch my breath because I was trying to choke down my emotions; they were pushing on my heart, making it hard to breathe. I got through my day, distracted by life, but I knew the emotions were still there, so I wanted to make sure I addressed my sadness before it got out of hand. Besides, I need to get ready for Italy, and I don't really want to take my emotions with me, even though I know I can't get away from them.

So, who am I without you? I am resilient, grateful, happy, loved, busy, sometimes sad, healing, forever grieving, going through life, figuring out how to do it without you, looking for romantic love, and a traveling fool. And I miss you so much it hurts. I kind of feel like saying I can't wait to see you, but that means I will be dead too.

Which is fine, but I have some living to do first. So, I will see you soon, and I will miss you every single day until I do.

Love,

Me

XOXO

PART V

LIVING LIFE AGAIN

115

Healing Grieving Heart

Yesterday, I was hanging out with Sam's husband, Steve, who is like a brother to me. He told me he has been depressed for the last year. I thought, *How can I not have seen this?* I spend a lot of time with him and his wife, but I had no idea. It threw me off, and the only thing I could think to ask was "Why?" I should have been able to figure it out myself, but he showed no signs. He was business as usual because that's who he is. Of course, Sam has MS, which is a big reason for his depression. It's a really fucked-up disease. They all are. But when you know it up close and personal, you just wish it didn't exist. I have two very close friends in my life with it, and they truly are the most positive women I know. They inspire me. Anyway, Steve told me he just wants his wife to be normal, but he knows she will never get better. Their love story is one I long for in my own life. They have been married for thirty years and are so in love. They laugh, they argue, they bicker, and they love! They are real. I didn't know what to say to Steve in the moment, mostly because men don't usually share that kind of emotional stuff. But I know what to say now....

They don't stay forever. That's it. They leave us. They go somewhere else, and it's called heaven. We get to go too. But if they go first, it feels like hell on earth. At first, it feels like you are dying too. And it may feel like your heart cannot withstand any more pain. In fact, it may feel like if any more pain is endured, it will stop beating too. It's unreal to feel that much pain. It's a debilitating feeling, and it can feel like you are sick because you are. Your heart is actually breaking. You probably will fall apart. But instead of dying, you actually wade the waters of the heartache and pain.

Then you realize that time has passed and you can get out of bed because that's who you are. You don't wallow. You get up. You wash your face for the first time, and your eyes see clearly again. You weren't sure any of this would ever happen because you just want to go be with your loved ones. But deep down, you know that's not how this works, and you know with every fiber in your body that you are not meant to lay down and die. You are meant to get back up and live. You still may want to go and not care, but you know you are not going anywhere. You are staying here on earth because you are not done yet. Something deep inside of you just knows. Somehow you figure out how to take a step. And then the day comes when you laugh again. And it feels so good because you didn't think it would ever happen again. Even though you cry almost every day, the pain lessens along the way. Each day, you step. Each day, you cry. Each day, you get back up and go to work. That's who you are. Because you are still here.

If you are here, there must be a reason. So you plod along and just know that God is leading you on your way. He must know more. He has sent angels to hold your heart in their hands. He has sent angels to guide you to the next step. They actually lead you to the people who will shelter you when you are grieving. They know who can handle a heavy heart. They will lead you to a place where you feel safe. Just like they led me to you and Sam. You both have made me feel safe along my journey of grief and healing. For this I am eternally grateful beyond measurable words. I didn't know it was happening along the way, but one day you said you thought I was never going to recover. I had no idea that was what you were seeing through your eyes. But you two never faltered. You just opened your doors, your home, and your hearts to me. And it seemed so natural—like family. It never felt like anything else. I felt safe. I felt sheltered. And to show my gratitude, I give back. I try to do yard work for Sam, to help you do the things around the house and keep the laughter out loud. Keep it real. And never, ever will I lose sight of who was there for me during the most challenging time of my life. It was both of you! You are my chosen family, and I am so grateful my angels led me straight to you. I did not realize until I wrote this how instrumental my friends were and are in my healing. I am profoundly and deeply breathing in gratitude. I am internally sobbing, yet feeling wonderful in my healing grieving heart.

116

Lari

Here we go again. My sister-in-law Lari was just diagnosed with liver cancer. No treatment. Just go home and call hospice. That's all they offered at the hospital. My brother Bobby and Lari just cried. She told him, "I'm not ready to leave you," and he isn't ready to lose her. My heart is breaking for them. This is a tremendous loss. Your wife is your chosen one. The family you get to choose. And now Bobby is having to come to terms with losing her. She was my only sister left. After Gayle got brain cancer and was fucked up after surgery, I truly felt that God gave us Lari to help fill the void. I am now beside myself and not ready to let go of my God-given sister. He gave her to me, and now He is taking her back. After my dad died, I told God there were to be no more deaths in my family for thirty years. I thought we had an agreement. Apparently, I was the only one who agreed. Did I mention I'm leaving in two days for the trip of a lifetime? I am going to Norway to see the Northern Lights, the number-one thing on my bucket list! Two weeks—a five-day cruise, dog sled ride, reindeer ride in a sleigh, and our last night is in a glass igloo in Finland! Now I'm thinking it's going to be a journey. An emotional one, and I will be thinking a lot about life and death and what I am here to do while I am on this earth.

The day my brother brought Lari home to meet our family was a *big* deal. He had been an alcoholic and addict for so long that we didn't think something like love would ever be a part of his life. When we met Lari, we instantly fell in love with her. She was warm, lovely, and loved my brother! She was easy and fun, and she blended into our kooky family effortlessly, despite our health issues and history. She was gold, and we knew she was a perfect fit for us all. She brought fresh air to our family, and we opened our arms to her liveliness!

I am struggling a bit with this decision to go on my trip because I am so used to dropping everything to go help my sister. Which is how I am going on this trip at all. I did drop things to go help my sister. My dad helped my mom and Dan took care of Gayle. It just seemed to be how it all flowed. When someone needed help, we just did what we needed to do. Now that they are all gone, I am living my life. Larger than I would have if they never went through the health issues they did. I would have lived status quo, not done anything out of the ordinary, because that's what my mom did; she lived life for everyone else. I figured out that we don't all live life that way. I also found out we don't live life selfishly either. We support, give, love, show up, and are strong. To me, there is no other way.

117

Bittersweet

I just went on the trip of a lifetime! I saw the Northern Lights, took a cruise through the Norwegian fjords, went on a reindeer ride, stayed the night in a glass igloo, and took in some of the most beautiful scenery I've ever seen. On the last night of my trip, I learned that Lari passed away. Now if that wasn't the wind coming out of my sails, I don't know what is. I love my sister-in-law so much.

The last time I saw Lari was two years ago. They live in Lake Havasu in Arizona. The drive is so long and I really don't enjoy it, and they stopped coming for the holidays. Still, I find it hard to believe two years have gone by. But my brother asked me to come visit for my birthday and I said yes. We went for a ride in their "side by side" and shot Dad's old guns and just hung out. We went to the casino and had a good time. Lari loved to play the slots, and she won while I lost, but it was all good. Just a reminder of why I would rather donate money than give it to a casino.

That weekend, I noticed a slowness to my sister. Finally, I asked my brother about it. He didn't know what was wrong. After I left, he asked her and she discovered her high blood pressure meds were causing her blood pressure to be too low. So the doctor took her off of her meds. Looking back at the photos I took, I think her body was shutting down. Years of smoking cigarettes, drinking wine, and not exercising likely took their toll on her fifty-six-year-old body. My dad said before he died, "She's gonna die from emphysema." At that point, I couldn't see a worse diagnosis. And I couldn't deny it.

Fast forward two years and I was about to embark on my bucket list trip. I was in a quandary the week before I left. I had two friends going with me who had never met each other, so I knew they would not go without me. Bobby and Lari both encouraged me to go. I went because I never imagined Lari would live less than two weeks. I knew in my heart I would be coming back to my sister dying. I was so wrong. She passed in less than two weeks from her liver cancer diagnosis. I am left in utter dismay.

I didn't find out until my last night in Finland. My brother didn't want to ruin my trip. He didn't even realize my trip was already over. I was leaving the next day, so my nephew let me know. I feel like I left my brother during the most difficult time of his life. His wife was dying, but I left for my trip. He dealt with a heavy hand. It is not easy to understand how he can deal with it, but he is. He is reeling. His heart is broken. He is learning how to breathe. Lari did everything for him. He is learning to be an adult all over again. Being the soul caregiver of their cats is a challenge but so good for his soul. He now has to take care of the household and feels overwhelmed. Overwhelmed by his emotions, his wife instantly gone, and how he is going to deal with it all emotionally, physically, and fiscally. And maybe family-wise? I don't know. He and Lari kind of stepped out of our family when our sisters and parents died. They just checked out. And now he is on his own to figure it all out for himself, and I fear his soul can't handle it. I fear my brother will be the next one to go.

I am not sure I can handle this reality. Whether it will be a year from now or thirty years, it will leave me with a huge empty place in my heart. He is my only immediate family left. That's it. Bobby and me. They are all gone. But our nephews and niece and their kids keep us going. It's all about the kids now. Children keep us all going and not just dying out.

118

Disbelief

Life can be heartbreaking. Life can break your heart. I don't know why it can or will, but I am one of the humans who got it broken. It broke when my sisters died. It broke when my parents died. Today, it broke over my sister-in-law dying. I wasn't ready for this one. Lari supported me in every way possible. She was my sister, my confidant, my friend, my family. After the rest of my family died, I thanked God for our new family member every chance I got. But it was time for her to go too.

Tonight, I am putting together her photos and writing her eulogy for her funeral. I am feeling numb. I still can't believe she is gone. I am in disbelief. The photos are making it real, and writing the words are simply breaking my heart again.

Humor and laughter have saved me up to now. And as always, I will go to my saving grace and put on my smiling face. Both feel so much better than the alternative.

119

Lari's Eulogy

Lari was my sister, my confidant, my family. She and I talked weekly. She blew into our lives like a beautiful bird and has now left in the same manner. I love my sister-in-law so much! I felt like she took the place of our sister Gayle after her brain cancer. Lari came into our lives just when we needed a bright light to shine. My brother came home with such a gleam in his eye when he met her. And we got to experience this wonderful, intelligent, and warm woman. We loved her from the moment we met her. She was fun, and she was just the right amount of kooky for our family. She fit right in, and I always felt like she filled a place in our hearts where our sister Gayle had left us.

The last twenty years have been so filled with ups and downs, but Lari always remained the same. She was our rock. When our family had health issues, she was there to help us figure out the best plan of action. She supported us in a way we never could have imagined. She was my "go to" girl whenever I had an issue or a fun thing to share because I knew she would help or enjoy the moment with me.

When Bobby and Lari bought their house in Lake Havasu, it was because they had quickly realized life was short, so why wait to get out of the rat race? They moved as soon as they could. They loved the lifestyle and what it offered, and they felt at home immediately. They made their house a home, and it was their happy place.

A whole bunch of cats later, I found out what an animal lover Lari was. She would collect food for the quails and bunnies and teach the cats to enjoy them…through the window of course. This was truly one of Lari's pure loves—the birds and animals. And they loved her right back!

My heart will always yearn for this woman, her quick wit, and how she helped to complete our family. I stand here today to say how blessed we are to have had this beautiful woman in our lives for even just a moment. And I am sad to say goodbye for now….

120

Cleanse

I woke up wanting to cry this morning. I feel an overwhelming sadness in my heart and can't put my finger on why. Of course, Lari's loss is first and foremost on my mind, but I also feel like my heart wants love so bad. I keep telling myself to focus on finishing this book because when that man comes into my life, I won't get it done. Most days, that advice works just fine, but today, I feel sad and weepy. Maybe it's from coming off my high of a trip of a lifetime to see the Northern Lights, or that the man I do have love in my heart for is not available. I feel confused about what to do first or next, so I sit here and write my feelings down, hoping this will help get it out of me.

I just went for my second cup of coffee and could hear the song "Don't Stop Believing" playing in my office, so I tried to focus on that. Don't stop believing. Then I remembered my Grandma Lottie showed up in my dream last night, which also made me sad. She was there to tell me Grandpa Louie had died. She was so sad and crying, and I didn't know how to comfort her. They say our loved ones visit us through our dreams, so I like that I got to see my grandma last night. She has been gone since 1988, but I have been told numerous times by psychics that she is always around me.

Ironically, she died before Grandpa Louie, so to see her lose him in my dream was sad on another level. I know I am all over the place writing this, but that's where I am right now. It's bugging me that I can't figure out what is bothering me. But I know a sad movie will pull it out of me and crying will cleanse my heart. Grief is a powerful and sometimes overwhelming experience. And I'm getting tired of it.

121

Live Life Now

All of a sudden, I have this tremendous urge to call my sisters. It came out of nowhere. Maybe it came from the music I'm listening to right now or the family photos I'm working on. I don't know. But it was real and overwhelming. Next week is Karen's birthday; she would have been fifty-nine. The last birthday I got to spend with her was her forty-ninth, and I look at that photo of us every day. I think of all the celebrations we never got to enjoy. We went through so many years of suffering and sadness, but we plodded along and put on our happy faces just the same.

Last night, I turned my calendar to see what the week ahead looked like and I saw that today was my sister Gayle's sixtieth birthday. I instantly started crying. There was no stopping those tears, so I just let them flow. All I could think was how all the things to celebrate went by the wayside a long time ago. Gayle was thirty-four when she got brain cancer, so it was so hard to celebrate the shell of my sister after that. After brain surgery, she was pretty much incapacitated and unable to take care of herself or her family. Her husband Dan had to step up and be the breadwinner and mom, as well as his role as father. He did the best he could, and we were all amazed by this man who obviously loved my sister with his whole heart. Gayle finally passed away from a stroke when she was fifty. Again, we never really celebrated that birthday because it was so hard to get excited about a life that was no longer being lived to its fullest, or even lived at all. She lost her short-term memory, so she wouldn't really know either way. My sister was gone long before she ever died, so we just waited for God to take her. I'm still sure He waited long enough for us to be able to let her go. February will be ten years since she passed, and that seems like so long ago, yet it feels like it was not long ago at all. My heart still aches, but I am still in search of balance in my life by having fun and traveling. "Live life now" is all I hear now in my head, and I can't help but think it's my family on the other side reminding me that it's okay to go on and to live.

My moments of sadness have lessened, making it a little easier to move forward and celebrate the life moments that are here to stop us from working and getting stuck in the daily grind. Life's milestones are there for a reason; they keep us living, and they are reminders that life isn't all about making money or working or pain and suffering. We need to stop and smell the roses along the way, and to celebrate life's biggest moments! We need to find joy and happiness in our journey while we are on this planet. Sixty is a big birthday, one neither one of my sisters got to celebrate, so I am here to take full advantage of every single day of my life, and I will find something to do today to honor my sister's big birthday. Happy Sixtieth Birthday, Sister! I miss your sweet, loving soul an awful lot.

As I stand here today, I wonder if the reason I want to call my sisters is because I am happy right now. So why am I crying? Life is good even though we lost our sister-in-law seven months ago. I recognize how important it is to live life now. That is my new mantra. Their untimely deaths remind me every single day to take the opportunities to go out and enjoy life, even if it's just going to a friend's house to visit and have a glass of wine. Next week, I am going to Yosemite, and last week I went to Lake Arrowhead with my friend's family. Taking the little opportunities and enjoying life is so important. One of my favorite songs is Keith Urban's "Wasted Time." It's about those summer nights and not really doing much, going nowhere, and how the best days of life were all that wasted time.... I find wasting some time is important—just relaxing, hanging out, playing games, and unplugging from work, computers, and my phone. I'm listening—keep sending me messages, my family.

122

Shaman

Today, my friend's brother was in need. Their dad passed away eleven months ago from cancer, and a lot of healing needed to take place. His wife left him five days after his dad passed, and his teenage sons turned their backs to him in a courtroom situation. Since then, I have learned a lot about their dad, whom I also knew. They are things you just don't share because you need to move on rather than let them ruin the rest of your life. I will leave it at that since it is not my story to tell.

But today, I watched a man who was falling apart, unable to pull himself together. So my friend called in a shaman, who is a super-cool dude named Nino. I learned today that a shaman is a spiritual healer. A spiritual healer is born with the ability, and it usually is carried on in families. I didn't know, so I asked. They do have to learn how to use their healing, and somehow, they sense it's there; they just have to find a teacher to show them how to use their innate ability. I didn't ask too many more questions because I didn't want to hinder what he was there to accomplish.

We started a caravan toward our local mountains. I thought I knew where we were going, but we headed in a direction I had not been, so I followed in my car, thinking I knew the path and we would be there in twenty minutes. I was wrong and followed them for over an hour to our destination. I love a good adventure! So when the paved road turned to dirt, I thought it was fun and unsuspected. Big holes in the road and running water in places were also fun, but only because they were very low, flowing creeks.

As I followed the brother's truck, I started tripping out when I saw his license plate read "Motivator." I thought how out of place this man must feel in his life to have thought he was a motivator and now he is lost. He is falling apart, unable to pull himself together because his heart has been broken in many ways—death, divorce, and abandonment. My heart started breaking, but I also know the heart can heal, and I needed him to know that. I had told him about my family dying and that I had felt hopeless and didn't care if I lived anymore. But I explained that if you live just one more day, everything changes.

Time truly is the only healer. It really is. And I want to say it again. Time is the only healer. I only know because it's been nine years since my sisters died, and I am in such a better place. I now know I need things to look forward to, like travel, seeing my family and friends, work, and whatever else interests me. I am completely changed from my life experiences. And I have found that I am okay. I strive not to let my past define me. This is important and hard to do.

We continued and finally arrived at the campsite where the healing would hopefully begin. We unloaded the truck and went on a hunt for willow and wood. I found it interesting that the shaman excused Mom first, then sister. I suggested sister (my friend) could drive me back to the campsite to get my car. The shaman explicitly said, "No." He said I would return to the campsite with him and his daughter because I wasn't finished yet. *Okay,* I thought. I was happy to continue.

Back at the campsite, we unloaded the wood and organized it for the week ahead that they would endure. Brother would be going on a vision quest. I don't even know what to think of this; he will be sent on his own to see his own vision. He will be alone for four days in the wilderness. And even though he agreed willingly and needs this, he was being a little combative, already pushing the shaman away. I can only imagine this will be a very uncomfortable, scary, growing, healing full of so many things I can't even imagine experiencing. A week without civilization.

I kept thinking, *Don't let another human break your spirit.* That is so important and something I would have never considered until my heart was broken by Jim. This man, my friend's brother who had his heart broken, has allowed two women to really mess him up. And then his kids are adding insult to injury. There's little difference between giving your heart to the Universe, to loving, to being who you are and not worrying if your heart gets devastatingly wounded and loving freely, and loving your loved ones completely. My best advice is just to do it. Every single time. LOVE. It is the greatest gift we get to feel on this earth. That's it. If you ever meet someone who doesn't know this and hurts your heart, just know love is still coming to you.

123

Obsessed or Ungrateful

I've been sitting here obsessing that this guy is ignoring me and that guy is disappointing me. I have been obsessed with finding love lately while being completely blind to what I do have. I am living life. I am traveling and doing things I never even thought about doing. I saw Cher and Earth, Wind & Fire in the same weekend. I just went skiing, and I saw the Northern Lights. Oh, and six months prior, I went to Italy, my first time abroad. I am also deciding on what kind of car to buy next, so I am feeling like an ungrateful idiot right now. I have it all in this moment. I have a home. I have friends. I have family. I have a business I absolutely love. And most importantly, I have my health. But here I sit wallowing in the fact that I don't have love.

Just because I have had loss doesn't mean I get to forget what life is really about. It's about experiencing all the good, all the difficult, all the loss, love, highs and lows, trauma, abuse, and family dynamics. And figuring out along the way how to manage emotions, health, love, no love, fun, and loss. My friends who have amazing love but suffer from major health issues make love look easy. Other friends have love and happy lives. Then I have friends who just make happiness out of what they have. That makes me smile. And that's why they are all my friends. I watch and learn from them. Even though I don't have love right now, I have so much! I have my friends whom I call my family. I have my family members who are becoming stronger together. And I have my wonderfully charmed life.

My heart has mended a lot in the last nine years. To want a certain love in my heart again is a true blessing, and I am so grateful. I always go back to God's plan for me. Even though I am a recovering Catholic, I truly know God has a plan.

124

Greatness

Sometimes, we know when we are in the presence of greatness. Last night, I was privileged to photograph an event in San Francisco. I got connected because of a friend who recently moved to the Bay Area and now works for a nonprofit that helps homeless families. The owner of the Giants baseball team was there, so there were some heavy hitters, no pun intended, present. But the one who stood out to me is a rabbi in

San Francisco who was honored at the event. It was beautiful and I'm having a hard time not tearing up recalling it. I knew nothing about him before, but I recognized he was a humble, sweet, fun, giving, loving, caring, grateful, wonderful man who was leading his congregation by example. Leading by example is something many of us forget to do while living on our cell phones and social media.

I cannot express how humbled I was to be in this man's presence. And I was amazed by how young he is. I would expect someone with such qualities to have more experience and have lived much longer. I was pleasantly surprised and so glad to have experienced such a great human spreading the message of love. The nonprofit supports homeless families in San Francisco. Homelessness is overwhelming our entire state and beyond. I can't imagine how to fix the problem. I don't feel like our government is even addressing it, so it makes me sad.

Last night, I saw some pretty awesome humans working on finding a solution. Now I see this non-profit has the blueprint to solve the problem and it can be duplicated. It just takes motivated people to start the process. I can see myself in the process, and it does not scare me. I am already in the process because I care and give food to individuals in need. I want to give back to our community and inspire others to do the same. You can give a little, or a lot. Just do it. We are all just one small moment away from being in a desperate situation, but perhaps we are also all the solution. Let's not wait for the government to fix this problem; it will take way too long. Let's step in as humans and help each other. Let's find solutions in each of our communities. Let's reach out to communities that have already started to help homeless families and find out what they have done that actually helps. Together, I believe we can do this because I have seen the results. We can be heroes.

125

Mia

One of my former wedding photography brides, my friend Connie, asked me to photograph her furry friend Mia. Mia is dying but still looks so beautiful, so she wants me to capture her in photographs. I immediately said, "Yes. I can come tomorrow!" I know how important our relationships are with our pets. It's been twelve years since Rufus died, and I still haven't replaced her. She was my child, and it broke my heart when I had to put her down. I still cry when I tell the story about the two days preceding her demise.

When I arrived, Connie looked so very sad and had tears in her eyes. I followed her to Mia. Mia has been Connie's beloved friend for eighteen years, and now she is almost ready to go to Kitty Heaven. I broke out my camera and settled in. I know it's important to let the animal come to me and let them be. They will always do what they want anyway, so don't stress them out by trying to force anything to happen for the camera. Letting them be is usually how something wonderful happens.

As we let Mia be, Connie told me her story about the night of the Montecito debris flow. I held myself together while she told her story. Connie said when the mudflow happened, she was alone with her two small children and Mia because her husband was away on a business trip. Connie lived on Olive Mill Road, about five houses above Coast Village Road. That is where all the mud and debris flowed down into what looked like a mud river, but it was actually her street. Thankfully, they lived in a two-story house and could flee upstairs. When she saw the "glow" from a fire, she went looking for Mia downstairs and wanted to make sure the doors were open so Mia could get upstairs to join them. She had no clue what was about to hit their home. A wall of mud flowed down their street and right into their lives, engulfing the entire first floor. It was creeping up the stairs, trying to take over. Mia made it upstairs, but the mud on her paws testified that she had waited till the last minute to find refuge with her family.

Connie said she heard fire truck after fire truck pass by her house early that morning to help all the other victims. Thinking the firemen would come to help her family too, she waited patiently, and eventually, they came and took them to safety. My favorite part is that when the firefighters scaled up to the second-story window, they took Mia first. They took the family cat first because she was ready to go and demanded it! "Meow," she said, and they said, "Okay, let's go" and put her in a basket and got her to safety.

Tonight, as I go through my photos of Mia, I can't help but cry. I can't help but cry as I retell Connie's harrowing story of the Montecito debris flow as she lived it. The whole thing truly upset me. It was devastating to the entire community, but I am amazed how much healing has taken place.

Unfortunately, Mia was euthanized a couple of days after I took her photos. I felt like the cat whisperer that day because she seemed mesmerized by me. She remembered how I used to feed her and hang out with her when Connie's family went out of town. During the photo session, I reminded her about when we met and how I would take care of her and we would play and she would have fun, even though her family was gone. I would tell her they were coming back soon so not to worry. Then I reminded her of how mad she was when the first baby was born. She would spray all over things to voice her disapproval! That was when she sidled up to me. After that, she never left my side that day. She gave me some of the most beautiful, relaxed expressions, and laid down right next to me. I had to switch to my phone at that point to capture this truly content kitty, living one of her last days on this planet. RIP Mia. My heart aches for Connie as she mourns the loss of her furry friend.

Losing our four-legged friends is such an emotional time. When times are good, bad, boring, exciting, calm, eventful, or uneventful, they are always there for us. Perhaps the most difficult time after they leave us is when we come home and they are no longer there to greet us. That is when I noticed the loss the most. It was so painful. Eighteen years is a long time. I believe our furry friends help prepare us for death, even though I believe there is no point in preparing for death because it will happen either way. But our most loved creatures help us get used to the idea of losing our humans. Why else do dogs and cats live so much shorter lives than humans? It's to help us figure out how to go on without them, and perhaps each other.

126

Seventeen Years

Seventeen years ago today, my brother-in-law Jim committed suicide. That day changed a lot of things, including that my sister Karen no longer worried that her husband could possibly take her down with him. Don't get me wrong; he was a good man. He was just mixed up in his head. I always loved him, but somewhere along the way, he got lost and ended up taking his own life.

That day, Jim left my nephew without a father. All I could do was support Karen and help her plan his funeral. She was having health issues of her own, and now we were all feeling the emotional loss of my brother-in-law. At the time, I don't even remember thinking about how to get my nephew through his dad's death. I think I left it to my sister. I don't remember. It was all so overwhelming, so I just did what I saw in front of me to fix, help, or support.

Today, my nephew has two daughters and a fiancée. They've been engaged for ten years. They had their first child three months before Karen died. I remember Travis telling me he wanted to get married before she died. I said, "You will have to do it very soon because she is not going to last very long." That day came and went, but now after ten years, he decided to make their marriage happen. They are getting married in two months, and I couldn't be happier for them! I feel like Karen and Jim are in cahoots to help him make this happen. I don't know what has held Travis back all these years, besides grief, learning to be a father himself, and love. But enough time and healing has passed that he is in a place where he can be open to having a complete family of his own. The very thought melts my heart and brings tears to my eyes. We have a wedding to look forward to! And I am so excited!

A psychic once told me that if you take your own life, you have to work very hard on the other side to get the chance to come back and live another life on earth. Then she told me my brother-in-law was working to find me love. I found that fascinating. I can't help but think he is helping me along the way to find someone to love. I am taking someone to my nephew's wedding, and I think that has something to do with Jim.

Seventeen years ago, I decided to turn my journal into a book to help others going through difficult times. I hope I made the right decision.

127

Reset

Sometimes, I feel like I fail daily. I wonder if I should just be forgiven automatically because of all the trials and tribulations I've been through. Then I realize I have to be the best human ever. Not everyone knows what I have been through, so if I am having an off moment, how would they know? They don't. That is why it is my responsibility every single day to be my best. Be humble. Be funny. Be inspiring.

This month—which happens to be all of this new decade so far, 2020—I haven't felt like I am in a positive place. I feel like I am in a funk. I didn't see it coming. I am guessing it is because this month is the ten-year anniversary of Gayle's death and Karen's will come four months later. As much as I think it no longer affects me, it does. I have been here enough times to recognize it. It is grief. It is what it is. I don't always see it coming, but I know it when it happens. And then I am humble because I become someone I don't even want to know. I know I am better than this, but I am back in the place I was way before my family died. I'm sick of this yucky fog that keeps creeping into my daily life and makes me think I'm being funny or sassy. It's nothing but me being a pain in the ass, and the sooner I fix it, the sooner I can go back to being happy with myself.

I honestly can't believe it's been ten years. The pain and pure angst are gone, but the huge hole in our now little family has never gone away. That makes me feel like time has not passed. I am right back in the place I tried to move on from before. And I behave badly. It's a vicious cycle. Except now I have added some highs and some adventures back into my own life. But I think about what I'd give to have my sisters back. I actually have not gone there until now because I realize it would be pure torture to think about it. I know I can never get them back, so to wish for it is complete insanity. I can't add insult to injury. So I just stopped myself right now. I can't let myself wish for something that will never be. That would be hopeless. I have lived in that space before and I didn't like it. I wanted to lie down and die. But I didn't. I fought and got back up. I got counseling. And I smiled again. I laughed, and I moved myself out of that place.

Right now, I realize all I really needed to do was cry. I just needed to cry. That's all. Cry. It always resets the pain, grief, angst, and unrecognizable person I become. Every single time.

128

Surviving

Today is the ten-year anniversary of Gayle dying. I'm not sure how I feel about this day. All I know is so much has changed. My heart has healed tremendously, which is something I wasn't sure I would ever say. But it's true. Time truly is the only healer. Today, I choose to be happy. Yes, there are still moments when I grieve. Now I don't even know what is wrong with me when it happens because it happens less frequently and is not as recognizable. The day Gayle died, I had no idea that four months later, I would also say goodbye to Karen. There is nothing like losing both sisters in such a short period of time. I couldn't believe God allowed it to happen. I felt I had lost control of my mind, but I knew I had to hold it together.

I'm not sure why I even cared about keeping my shit together. I just did. For my parents, for my nephews and niece. Everyone was on their own trying to figure out how to handle such a horrific situation. People tried to warn me it was coming. I will never forget when Sunny, my ex-boyfriend Joe's sister, randomly blurted out, "Your sisters are going to go really close together." And they did. I figure she receives messages from the other side like I do from time to time. I really listened to her that night. I knew she was getting this information from somewhere else. But I never could have imagined all that happened would. It didn't matter. There was no way to prepare for it. Even if I knew the future, it would not have mattered. I would not have been able to cope any better than I did. I often tell friends who are dealing with aging parents, there is no way to prepare. Just be with them as often as you can. You will never regret the time you spend with them while they are here.

I just realized I regret how much time I didn't spend with Gayle. It was so hard to see her as she was. She wasn't my sister in the space she was for so many years. I missed her a long time before she left this planet. We all did. No one knew how to handle the loss. The loss was right before our very eyes. We knew she was never coming back. And then she died.

The four months that followed were such a trip. I tried to save my other sister's life by fundraising to buy the Poly-MVA that she believed was making her better. But it was too late. Her body was dying. It was a toss-up between giving her hope and spending time with her during her last days. So many of my friends came together to help. They brought all kinds of stuff for a huge yard sale. So much stuff that I held it two weekends in a row. And I could have had one hundred more! We raised $4,000 in two weekends, and my sister was so touched by all the people who wanted to help. I went the next weekend to be with her. She only had five weeks of life left. I will never regret the time I spent with her. It was horrible and loving and painful and nothing I ever wanted to do. But I did it. I did it all with love in my heart because I knew what was about to happen, and I had no idea how it would affect the rest of my life.

I know now. I know I am strong. Resilient. A fighter. Compassionate. Loving. Sassy. Salty (I was just told recently). A matriarch. Reliable. Sensitive. An aunty. A giver. An adventurer. A worldly traveler. Fun. And most of all, I have overcome the most insurmountable tribulation of my life. So I guess I am a survivor. Someone recently told me I need to change my words from "I was behaving badly" to "I was behaving appropriately for my experience." I will not let myself off that easily, but she was adamant about my change of wording when I talk about myself. I guess my experience is an unusual one, but I can only learn by it. I am still here and I will strive to be the best I can always be. I have a hard time letting myself off easy when "I behave badly." Those are my words and how I feel, but when someone sets me straight and basically says to give myself a break, I listen.

129

Losing My Friend

It's officially spring. I can see the new green buds outside on the trees and green is everywhere. Spring means new life, but right now, it has all new meaning. My friend Ari seems to be at the end of her life, and it is breaking my heart. I knew this was the end result of her MS, but I am not prepared or ready to deal with it.

The world is going through the coronavirus pandemic right now, and I've never seen nor heard of anything like it happening before. Most of us will be okay in the end, but in the meantime, it is killing our elderly and anyone with an immune system issue. It's highly contagious and Italy is having a difficult time getting through it. Some say they didn't react fast enough, which is why most of the US is under orders to shelter in place and avoid contact with each other. A small price to pay to help stop this pandemic. It is surreal and sometimes lonely, but thank God for FaceTime to help us feel connected. It's raining right now, which makes me want to stay inside and hunker down, so it's nice that the weather is cooperating.

Back to Ari. We grew up three doors down from each other, so I have known her my whole life. We were thick as thieves growing up, and we got back together as adults. She trusted me with her disease because she knew I could handle it after my family died. The last time I saw her was at Christmas three months ago. She was weaker, and it was harder for her to talk. I was my "funny" old self, trying to be light and fun, but this time it didn't go the way it normally did. She called me out and said I was trying to be funnier and have a better story to tell. *Fuck*, I thought. *I am just trying to bring humor and fun to you because I know what a fucked-up disease is in your body.* I handled it much better than I ever thought I could. I knew it was hard for her to talk, so I owned my shit, took it like a biotch, shut my mouth, and let her speak her truth. I felt terrible. And I didn't want that to be our last interaction.

She felt bad and texted me a few days later, and I gladly texted back. But I knew. I knew she was getting weaker, and that's why she was frustrated. But I never said I was sorry. If I don't get the opportunity now, I will truly regret not having done so. When they say life is fleeting, it is. Don't take it for granted. Not ever. Just assume the loved one you wronged will not be here tomorrow and you will never get to tell them how stupid you feel for being your own stupid self. Imagine never getting to say I'm sorry. Imagine them dying and you never get to right the wrong you feel you wanted to right in your heart before they went to the other side. Just imagine. I am imagining it right now. It is a lesson I have already learned so I am now so disappointed in myself.

I cannot pray that she lives another day in her fucked-up, debilitated, unable-to-move-her-body state just so I can say I am sorry and I love you. She knows. But I will live the rest of my life regretting. And I don't believe in living in regret. But I am right now.

I wish I had done things differently. I said yes to coming to take care of her next month so her husband could go to the lake for the weekend. But he cancelled because Ari wasn't doing well. I was still planning on going down to see her and spend time with her. She didn't know; I was going to surprise her. Now I wish I would have let her know. It's possible I will still have the chance, but that means they will have to put a feeding tube in if she doesn't pass away sooner. All I know is it's not really living anymore. She enjoyed eating and having a little wine. Now all the fun is in the past.

Ari's MS has taken its toll on her body, and the other day, she aspirated on food while she was eating, which turned to pneumonia. She is now in the hospital. I can't believe how this is playing out. Because of the coronavirus, the hospitals are on lockdown and no visitors are allowed, not even her mom, husband, and kids. I can't believe she is there alone, without her loved ones surrounding her. I am dumbfounded that after a twenty-year battle with this horrible disease, we can't be near her. The hospital let her husband know that if she gets worse, the family will be notified and allowed to see her. What a terrible phone call that would be. Her kids, who are nineteen and twenty-three, are in complete shock and don't know what to do. They just sit there unable to move. Claire, the oldest, is taking care of Grandma, who is one of my "moms," and who is eighty-two and has COPD. She was just released from the same hospital as Ari with her own complications. She is at high risk of dying from coronavirus so they sent her home. We are all distraught with not seeing Ari. I cannot believe this is happening.

Pink Floyd's song "Wish You Were Here" just came on, and I am now crying. I am in uncharted waters in losing my friend. Until now, it's only been family. I do not know the complications of losing a friend. I am sad. I am sad for her family to lose such a bright light. I am sad for us all to lose such a bright light. She has been such a positive inspiration through this whole thing. They intubated her this morning. All she can do now is blink and nod to let them know she is okay. I'm cried out tonight and have nothing else to express. I am plopping and staring at the TV and hope my friend knows I am thinking and praying for her.

130

Being Sick

Being sick will change you and everyone around you. It's a profound experience, and any emotion can happen and will—fear, love, sadness, anger. You will experience amazing acts of kindness and shocking and non-supportive behavior. It all comes and everyone in the room will either become a sucker, a giver, or a stabilizer at any time, at any moment, on any given day. The reality is life is happening and is going to happen. The only thing you can do is show up. Show up with love. Show up with compassion. Show up with a positive attitude. Leave your own baggage at home. There is no room for it when a human is fighting for their life. Only that person whose life is on the line gets to fear, be angry, love, and experience all the amazing acts of love, compassion, and kindness from everyone around them.

Most people should know this, but either they don't or they forget. I don't know why; it seems pretty basic to me. When you are watching a life fade away, you would think everyone would know how to behave. Instead, they bring in their own emotions. I know their emotions are real and running high, but why would you want your loved one to have your issues be some of their last memories on earth? Why wouldn't you just set your own stuff aside during this truly devastating time and behave and give the last moments of your loved one's life some peace? I learned from my family that there are times when we must behave and make the best out of a situation, especially during the holidays. For some reason, my dad would always behave during the holidays. Thank God because my childhood would have been so much worse otherwise. This became a basic lesson for me.

Travis and his wife now decorate their house for the holidays with Karen's things, which I love! I know she is there when I see all of her decor. I love that Maddie honors my sister and her husband's mom by using Karen's things in their home. This is heartwarming, and I am so grateful that Maddie gets how meaningful it is. Travis is now a successful businessman, and I am so proud of him and my other niece and nephew for their resilience. They have been through a lot. It has been a difficult road, but they are doing well. I was in my forties when I lost my parents, but my niece and nephews were teenagers or younger when their lives changed. I feel lucky I had my parents until my forties, but it's hard to lose them at any age. Now I see my friends dealing with their aging parents, some of whom have Alzheimer's or cancer. My former in-laws are getting up there in age, which is hurting my heart. They are still my in-laws, and some of my only parents left. I see their age getting the best of them and I think, *If only I could be as lucky. Lucky to live to a ripe old age. Lucky to have lived a great life. Lucky to have each other for so many years!*

I'm still working on loving someone until I die, but I am okay with what I got. I have love in my heart, and that's enough for me. We don't always get to choose our paths, but I have King, my beautiful dog, whom I love so much. I chose to find him because I have so much love to give, and finding a man at this point isn't so easy, so I chose to find a different kind of love. It worked. I'm in love!

Writing this book has been cathartic and amazingly healing, but finishing it is so hard because I have to go back and remember all the suffering and pain. It's been a year since I have worked on it. I blame it on King, but tonight as I write, I see clearly how hard it still is to live all these events over again. Every emotion is right there on the surface of my heart, and feeling it takes me back to the moment when I was living it. To finish this book, I will have to compartmentalize it. Take one day each week to feel it and deal with it so I can continue to heal. At least that is my plan today. A psychic told me my book would save lives. That is my driving force. Nothing could be sweeter. I guess I need to tell my heart to keep healing.

131

Living During a Pandemic

It's Christmas Eve 2020, and I am spending it home alone. Well, almost alone. I have a twelve-week-old puppy, so I am not completely alone. COVID-19 has kept our family from trying to get together, just to be safe, which is more important than anything. But it has left me feeling sad and lonely for the biggest holiday of the year. I remind myself I have my little furry friend who has stolen my heart, and I feel real love for my furry child, but I am sad not to spend it with my family for the first time. This is a new place for me, and I don't like it. I'm teary-eyed and feeling sorry for myself. It's the worst I have felt since the giant hole in our family was created when my sisters died.

This year has been such a trip. No one saw it coming. It has changed our world so much. The pandemic has shifted everything. Personally, I feel like some good has come from it because we are going back to the basics—family, spending more time at home with each other, and slowing down the whole rat race we all live by. The traffic has become nonexistent, the oceans are healing—it's kind of like a global karmic cleansing.

So, back to feeling sorry for myself and wishing I was with my family on Christmas. I have reminded myself of how much I have! I have a home, great friends, my family, my beautiful puppy, my business, and most of all, my health! I have it all! I have *so* much! People are suffering financially, have no food, and are dying, but I am sitting here having a stupid pity party. I have lived through my life's truly difficult times, and I am humbled by them. I am living during a pandemic, and I am so grateful to understand how lucky I am. I truly have a charmed life and understand how important each and every happy morsel is that I get to experience!

Tonight, I am playing with my puppy, who has no idea that it's Christmas Eve, and even when I explain it to him, he doesn't care. Today is just a day in our lives, and who cares that it's a holiday? I love this little guy more than I could have imagined! I have never given birth, but I now have true respect for all mothers! He keeps me running all day! He poops and pees everywhere! We go outside and he goes; we go inside and he goes again! When I'm cleaning pee over here, he's pooping over there! It's exhausting, but I feel so loving in the moment. I love him so much, and I am so grateful for this soul to be in my life. He snuggles up beside me with his smooshie little face and kills me with cuteness every day!

With a new year right around the corner, I hope everyone can have a wonderful holiday and make the new year full of hope and love. We never know what the future holds. The only thing we can control is our attitude. My wish for us all is to always find the positive in every situation. I look forward to thriving in 2021, and I can't wait to see what the future holds!

I find it so important to look forward to something every day. To make plans and plan trips. Because without something to look forward to, I will just stagnate and go to that place in my head I should never go to alone. Life can be tricky, and I know where I am now is so much better than in my past. I just have to remind myself to adjust my attitude and love my life, and if I don't love my life, to ask myself, "What can I do to make changes?"

The inspiration is out there. You gotta pay attention because it can come from anywhere—a quote, a movie, a friend, a stranger. Look for it. It is there for you. Your angels are everywhere, and they want to help you through your life. I love it when I hear from my angels. I also have to pay attention because I can miss their messages if I don't. If time passes and I feel like I am not hearing from them, it's because I am closed off or in a dark place. Sometimes they really fight to get me the message when I am in the space of grief, darkness and sadness. For this, I am truly grateful. That I can receive a message from them is remarkable. That I can receive the message when I am in a difficult place is immense, and I will take it every single time. Now I especially look for the messages when I am in a space I don't know how to get out of.

All I can do is look forward. Look forward to the future. Look forward to the fun my puppy can provide me every day. Look forward to being alive another day. Whenever I get another day that exceeds my sisters' years, I am truly grateful. I understand that each day I get to live here on earth is a gift, and I don't take it lightly. I delight in going out in nature. I enjoy spending time with my friends, and I understand how lucky I am to live another day. I am happy to be alive. I don't know what the future holds, but I know I better live every day I get to the fullest!

And can I say that we are all going to die. It's those of us who get left behind who get fucked up when we least expect it. Although I saw it coming, it didn't matter. I felt obliterated. I have no words to express how I still feel to this day. Oh yes, I felt distressed, sick in my heart, dark. I was dark. But I am here to say I am in a much better place. I am still healing, but I feel so much better, and I see that my path is so much happier. I am happy again, and I can only thank my angels and time for my healing.

Tonight, I completely and truly understand what a charmed life I have. I was loved as a child, received an education, live in a free country, and have work I love. To forget those things makes me feel like a spoiled and loved person. Just because life didn't go as I imagined doesn't entitle me to feel sorry for myself. I may have felt that way at certain times, but time has healed and moved me forward. Others like my brother have inspired me. At this point in my healing, I cannot solely look back at all of the pain in my heart. I have to look forward to what lies ahead.... For that revelation, I am grateful. Perhaps having these revelations is what keeps me alive and going.

We don't know how our lives will turn out, but if you don't show up equipped for this wild ride, it can take you for a loop or two. Our attitude is all we truly have control over, and sometimes it's hard to be in control of that. Life will be what it is, and we have to accept it; however, we can do so much to make someone else's life a little easier, a little better, a little softer. Give some food to a homeless person, call a friend going through a difficult time, or just smile at a stranger. The little things can make a big difference. I'm not perfect, as many can attest to, but I know what it feels like when a friend shows up at my door because she knows my dog died or to make me breakfast because my dad died. Showing up for a friend is huge and, undoubtedly, what I remembered most when I was going through the hardest times of my life.

Tonight, I watched the movie *The Way We Were* for the first time. How could I have never seen it before? The film's song says that what's too painful to remember we choose to forget. Instead, we remember laughter. Well, I remember all of it. The pain, the sadness, the laughter, and all the suffering I witnessed. I miss them all. I don't miss the pain, the sadness, or the suffering, but I do miss my family an awful lot. I am grateful for the family I have, and I am so grateful for our bonds—we truly love each other. I am so grateful my brother has come so far with his healing heart. Today, he spoke about how he may not want to find love again because of how his heart was broken when Lari died. I simply cannot deny him having that thought.

As I sit here with my puppy, whose life will only last a mere decade or so if I'm lucky, I can only focus on now and feel all the love and joy I have in this moment. I know my furry child won't live forever, but I chose to have one now, and I won't look back on not having him. I have so much love to give and I choose to give it to my furry child. I hope everyone gets the opportunity to love a furry friend because they give it right back and unconditionally. Don't get me wrong; they are a lot of work! So, if you don't have the time and resources, help a friend with theirs or go help at a shelter or even foster one. You won't regret it.

132

Feeling Inspired

It's been three-and-a-half years since my sister-in-law Lari died. Since then, my brother has done nothing but inspire me! About three months after she passed, he quit smoking! They both smoked. He really wanted to quit again, but it was not easy when that was something they did together. He did it before, but when he fell off the wagon, he started smoking again. He always said that quitting smoking was way harder than quitting drinking alcohol. He couldn't get over how easy it was this time to quit smoking! He said he ran out of cigarettes one day and simply decided not to buy anymore. He couldn't believe he wasn't crabby, and trust me, he can get crabby. That was it. He was done smoking.

About nine months after Lari passed, he called me and said he wasn't feeling right. *Oh no,* I thought. *Please, God, let's not go to this place! I am not prepared to lose my brother and only immediate family member left.* I asked Bobby what he meant. He said he felt like he wasn't eating well. I thought, *Okay, we can work with this,* so I asked him if he thought he could add a salad every day to his diet. He said yes, and every time I talked to him, he was eating or making a salad! I was so proud of him, even inspired.

Two years after Lari passed, he started complaining about pain in his stomach. *Oh no,* I thought again, and I immediately started praying to God. I asked God to let this be something that can be corrected with food. Once again, God answered with diverticulitis. What a relief! I was so happy to hear it wasn't something more serious. So we started looking into what to eat and what not to eat. Again, he inspired me. He cut out coffee, dairy, and a few other things, and his stomach is a lot better. Again, I am so proud of my brother and his determination to better his life and health.

My brother turned sixty last year. He noticed how his body was unable to handle the heat in Lake Havasu anymore. He was cramping so bad it was debilitating. He couldn't work and decided he had to make a change. He sold his house and moved to a cooler part of Arizona. He has a friend who is like a brother to him, who lives near Prescott, and they are going to paint houses together. My brother went to visit his friend and look at homes for sale. He found one that wasn't built yet and put a deposit on it, then went home to start the process of selling his house he has been in for eighteen years. In eighteen years, one can collect a lot of stuff. When our dad died, just the two of us were left to clear out the house we grew up in. Our parents had lived there for more than fifty years, so there was *a lot* of stuff! I worked on the attic and my brother pretty much did everything else. We donated, threw away, or kept certain things. I was careful not to keep too many items. I know it's just stuff, but it was important to me to keep things that reminded me of our lives or of my mom and dad. I kept three old-fashioned oil lanterns my dad collected and my mom's fifties-style green luggage—only the two smallest pieces because the big ones were huge. Other things too. My brother, on the other hand, loaded up his truck every time he was there, and it ended up being a storage unit full. Lari would call and ask me why I let him. I laughed and said I had no say over what he did. It was clearly part of his grief process. She agreed, so he got a storage unit to house all the treasures.

Thankfully, he eventually realized he didn't need everything he took home and gave it away or just let it go. His grief had lessened and he was okay not having all that stuff. He went through his garage and house for months getting rid of things he did not use or need to keep. He had a new outlook on life, and it was a relief to know he was healing. Then because he was ready to move to a new town, he was also ready to go through Lari's things, powered through, and got it done. He lifted the heavy weight of grief and sadness because he was finally ready. Again, I was so proud and inspired by my brother.

After Lari died, he started calling me more. At first, he was sad and lost without her. His cats helped him along the way; he had to care for them and they brought him happiness during this truly difficult time. He also reconnected with a girl he took to Disneyland in eighth grade. My brother doesn't own a computer, but shortly after Lari died, he finally got a smartphone. He discovered Facebook and loves finding old friends from our childhood. That is where he found Annemarie, his eighth grade Disneyland date. They have been talking for three years now and have become great friends over the phone. I think they are getting closer to meeting in person, and I know my brother looks forward to that day.

I am so happy his heart is healing and that he and I have become so close. We talk more than once a day, and I love it. It reminds me of when Karen and I used to talk for hours every day. Bobby and I are on the phone for at least ninety minutes a day. And I love each and every minute. It warms my heart to get so close to my brother. He tormented me as a child, but that's what older brothers do. One thing he would do is tell me I had to come into the bathroom to see a huge spider, only to lure me in to smell something awful. I still laugh at his antics to torture his little sister. He is my only family left from my childhood. He remembers things about our family I never knew, and I love that he shares them with me.

Bobby is a remarkable man to me now, even though he got the short end of the stick when it came to our dad. Dad picked on my brother and said some pretty shitty things to him on a daily basis, trying to make him a better man, but it only broke my brother down. He became an alcoholic and addict, but he found his way. One New Year's Day, Bobby woke up and decided he didn't want to drink anymore. So he stopped and got help. He still goes to AA and highly recommends the Twelve Steps even if you aren't an alcoholic. I need to go look them up and start living like my brother because he is a better man for it. I am inspired every day by him, and I can't wait to see what the future holds for him and me. I love my brother so very much, and I had no idea we would become so close. For this, I am grateful.

133

Dying People

I am overwhelmed right now. Tomorrow is the twelve-year anniversary of Karen's death, and I just found out that three vibrant young women have died. One I knew as an acquaintance through other friends, one I hardly knew, and the third I knew professionally but thought she was a kick in the pants. The one I knew through friends was Rachil. She was diagnosed with breast cancer and wanted to do sexy photos for her husband, so we did the session and she was so much fun to photograph. Alive, vibrant, and lovely are words that best describe her, and she had a great time too. She was an acupuncturist and decided to treat her cancer naturally, which I completely understand. I can't say I would treat it any other way after I saw what chemo and radiation can do to a body. She didn't want to give it energy, and I felt the same way.

Two years later, Rachil is now gone. She got COVID, which really weakened her, and she passed away. Before she went to get treatment in Mexico, she told me, "If I don't come back, please make the photo album for my husband." I hadn't heard from her in a while and didn't want to bother her while she was trying to heal, so I decided to get it going. I was about to email her when the very next morning, Julie, my friend whom I met Rachil through, texted me that Rachil had passed—the day before I started working on the album. I thought she must have somehow reached out to me energetically to get the album done. At least that's how I felt. I worked on it for a week and I cried every time I saw Rachil's beautiful face. I couldn't believe this bright light was no longer on this earth. I don't know why death still affects me this way. I would think I've experienced enough of them to be a little jaded. I'm not. It still really sucks. And it makes me sad and I cry. She was a lovely person, and I got that. I started thinking about her sisters and parents and husband, and that's when I really lost it. It took me right back to when my sisters died and the huge heartache my parents experienced. It was horrible to witness. I guess I know it all too well. The huge hole in my black heart was so impossible to handle. Imagine that. A black heart with a hole! Unimaginable. It was so very hard, but I kept on, and eventually, I was able to laugh again, love again, and experience life with gusto.

I still need something to look forward to, and right now it's a trip to Hawaii. Also, my heart is full with the love I feel for this little guy named King. He is "adorsables," as my brother likes to say, and I love it. He was five pounds when I got him, and now he's almost thirty. He has stolen my heart too, and I am so grateful for all the love I feel for him. He gets me through people dying. I look at him and can't stay sad for very long. I might revisit feeling sad, but he pulls me out of any ill feelings. I can't stay in that place for very long. For that, I am eternally grateful.

Today was when I learned the other two women had passed. I was shocked. One was forty-four and the other was probably around fifty. One left a nine-year-old and the other a teenager. I'm so very sad for those kids. I couldn't help thinking the apocalypse came for them sooner than they would have thought. Why did these young, beautiful women have to go now? Perhaps God is bringing the good ones home to help Him get ready for all the souls from the end of the world. I don't know; I'm talking out of my ass right now, but who really knows? I certainly don't. Actually, I don't want to know. I would rather just keep on living life for now. When it's over, it's over, and I hope my regrets will be few. I already have a few, so I will work on not adding more. Live life now! It's my mantra and hashtag. Care to join me?

A FINAL NOTE: SOARING

I'm in Italy writing my last chapter. I know it's my last chapter because in my heart I know it's time to move on with the rest of my life. It's time to let go of the sadness and grief. I know it will always be there, but for now, I need to put it in my pocket and keep it there safe and sound. As I sit here gazing at the most beautiful, spring Tuscan landscape, I realize how vulnerable I am. It's been twenty years now since I began writing this book, and I feel the need to get it done! I came to Tuscany to get it done and have this beautiful experience in Italy. Today, in the morning light, I'm reflecting on my journey. I am putting pressure on myself now, and I intend to send the book off to the editor when I get home.

So far, this trip has had a common theme, and the funny thing is, I already wrote it! My book coach told all of his author clients that we are earth angels and God will give me the passion to finish this book. We are all here to act on our soul mission and goal, and this process is not just writing a book. I am living out my soul level mission as an earth angel.

Yesterday, I took a two-hour yoga class with an amazing instructor named Francesca. She lives on a four-hundred-year-old estate that used to be a monastery. It was amazing! She showed us the wine cellar the monks used to make wine in. She and her husband have carried on the tradition. An inscription was carved into the stone wall that she had translated. I can't remember it all, but it was about wine and prayers for the success of the grapes.

The instructor talks and teaches throughout the yoga session, and I felt like she was speaking directly to me. Things like, "Get rid of what does not serve you and release it. Be open to new patterns and raise your vibration. It's up to you how you want your life to be. Chop off dead old branches of old patterns and leave them behind with *joy*. Victim mentality does not serve" (actually victim mentality drives me nuts!), and my favorite, "Be the beautiful self you are for the rest of your life." I couldn't believe all the things she said, and I ate it all up! I felt like she said what I have figured out in the twenty years of healing and grieving, and it was so beautiful to hear her say it all in one space. I got emotional when I threw what does not serve me over my head and behind me to let it go, and my body felt so much better when we were done. I must continue with the practice of yoga when I get home because of how it made me feel.

After the class, she shared a wonderful spread of food and sparkling wine. She shared her writings, which I found so special. They were creative cards, and she had water-colored the background and then written things from her heart. One of my favorites was: "I promise myself that I will enjoy every minute of the day that is given me to live."

So, back to what this is about.... I have learned through so many experiences, and I will never stop learning. I have learned how much I miss my family every single day. I still cry over the loss of them. I don't believe that will ever go away. I have learned not to subject myself to people who do not bring out the best in me. My ex Jim and I are still friends because he brings out the best in me. I learned if I don't have to cut someone off, then I shouldn't just because our relationship didn't work out. We are friends again, and it's wonderful to talk to someone who still brings out the best in me. I have also learned that friends come and go, and that's okay. I have learned to let them go.

I have also learned that you gotta spread the dread. When life gets tricky, it's important not to unload on the same person; that gets old for a human, and it's important to talk to different friends. It may give a new perspective, and it may make it clear who are your real friends. I have also found that when you're the only one taking care of yourself, you gotta pay attention. It doesn't cost anything. Seriously, I have to make sure I am taking care of myself when my heart is feeling sad or obliterated. I find it helps if I get a massage, go for a walk, call a friend who gets me, and take care of my heart and soul. Whatever it takes to make me feel better. Oh, and I was always taught that after laughing comes crying. My mom always used to say that, but I believe it's the opposite—after crying comes laughing! And it feels *so* much better. But then crying will come again, and then it becomes a cycle, and that's a good thing because it helps balance out life.

I have learned that when thinking about how my parents may have messed me up, I have two options: I can stay angry at them and be miserable for the rest of my life, or I can just let it go and be happy. I choose happy almost every time. I know that sounds easy, but sometimes it is not. But I go back and do things to take care of myself. And now that my parents are gone, I can't stay mad at anything that happened. I can only use it as a learning experience and move forward with the rest of my life because I am here for a reason.

I have learned that I am never too old to grow. And a smile always inspires a smile. And microwaves change the molecular structure of food. I'm not sure what that means, but it can't be good, so I use mine sparingly. I have also learned that energy can shift on a dime, and my life can change in a second—sometimes in a positive way, and sometimes in a negative, stressful, or sad way. Learning how to deal with this is when I need to dig deep into my heart and soul to look for a positive outcome. Sometimes when I was in the thick of it and watching my family suffer and die, I fell apart. I was unable to see the lesson. I was going down, and it was a long way down. But I found that getting up was so much harder than going down. Going down is easy. No one expects much from me when I am experiencing a loss. But when the smoke clears and I can take a step forward, it's not always easy to be the person I want to be. Because the pain and loss are still there, and they never really go away, but it's how I figure out how to move through it while navigating my way through life, people, and friendships that matters.

Someone once said it's better to feel pain than never feel at all, and the opposite of love is indifference. I think it's from a Lumineers song. When I think about indifference, knowing it means lack of interest or concern, mediocrity, I know I can't live my life like that. Having no passion about the things I love is almost like a punishment to me. It's like being numb to life, and I can't live like that. Instead, I choose to live life now! And that feels so much better. Even if I have to go through the rest of my life without most of my immediate family. If I'm not going to choose happiness, then I should just go now.

So, here I am in Italy, choosing to live my life. I know my family is always with me, guiding me, supporting me, loving me from the other side, and that is how I go on. I've seen 11:11 on the clock a few times already, so I know they are reassuring me they are here with me. My brother called me and wanted to know all about Italy and the five-hundred-year-old villa we are staying in. I love how close he and I have become. I never saw that coming! It's the best thing to have my only immediate family member so close to me now; it warms my heart. We are always sharing stories about our family, and I love it. Even though it's taken me twenty years to get here, I will never wish for another life.

I find flowers make me smile, so I make sure I buy them for myself a lot. They are part of taking care of myself, so I almost always have them in my space. I wish I could have all my soulmates in one place. It's a cool thing once I identify them. I meet them and instantly get along with them even at a very young age and then—boom! Forty-nine years later, we realize we still really like each other and we are still friends. I make sure I turn my tragedies into triumphs. Someone once dared me, so I took the dare and here I am.

I find it's important to change and keep evolving. Otherwise, I can become boring and monotonous. Boring and monotonous are two things I want nothing to do with. I must keep moving forward. My little furry friend was a big change in my life. His little soul has changed me for the better, and I can't believe how much love I have for him in my heart. I miss him so much while I am away. I am his human, and I just hope he is okay until I return home. I kept telling him I would be back and it's only twelve days. I have to keep living my life, so I had to go, and I feel I have left him with the best care I could find, but I still love, miss, and worry about that little guy. He too has stolen my heart, and I am so thankful he is in my life. I know my time is limited with him, so I don't take it for granted, and I now know how to live through heartbreak. I still don't like it, but I know it's a part of life, and we don't get out of here alive, no matter how much we love. I just hope it transfers to the other side and we will be together forever. I do not look forward to that day, but I know it's inevitable. I try not to go there in my mind and just enjoy him today. Today is all we have. Live for today because tomorrow may not come.

I wouldn't be here if it weren't for my experiences. Even though my childhood was difficult, I realize my life is truly charmed. I have a family who loved; even though we were dysfunctional, we figured it out. We had each other. We used humor to get through difficult times as well as everyday life. My dad mellowed with age, making it easier to forgive him. As I said before, he told me when he was forty that he went through a mid-life crisis and behaved very badly. I was glad he felt the need to explain himself. Oddly enough, he died at eighty, which made forty truly the middle of his life. Somehow, he must have known deep down in his soul. I have learned many times that I must be present to win. I actually love that part of myself. I can have something terrible going on, yet when I am enjoying what I am doing, I have the ability to stay in the moment, and I can forget for even just a little while what was happening in my life.

I have now left Tuscany and found my way to Venice. I wanted to see a new part of Italy. It was Labour Day weekend in Italy, and it was crowded. I'm not a big fan of crowds, but the moment I stepped off the train, I was mesmerized by this beautiful, ancient city surrounded by waterways. I'm pretty sure my mouth was open as I took it in, but I didn't care. I was only there for two nights, so I wanted to see everything amazing and experience all there was to see.

The next day, I went shopping with my new friend CoCo. We walked for miles, dodging the crowds. After hours of taking it all in, we were completely exhausted. So, we went back to our little apartment and plopped down. We were chatting when, all of a sudden, my family showed up! Not visually, but energetically. And they came with messages for me. CoCo is apparently psychic, and they were going through her. I had no idea. The first thing they wanted me to do was to stop living my book! It's over and they are at peace, and they don't enjoy watching me hold on to grief. Holding on to grief is not holding on to them. It's a disservice to them when I grieve so deeply and they start feeling heavy. They want me to let it go. And to let the butterflies fly! They told me to change my words from "I miss them" to "I love them." Only joy now! No more sadness. It has to be a conscious awareness, and I have to choose to let them go. They love what I am doing by traveling, and it's time to live now. My dad wanted me to know he is deeply sorry for how he behaved during his life. They told me to be forgiving and quit harboring resentment; it's not important. They want me to know they are always with me. They said I have done a very good job of writing this book and that I wrote it. I have felt for a long time that I channeled it, but I guess it was all me. I'm not sure how to let them go just yet, but if I am supposed to make a conscious effort, I will start today. I don't want their souls to feel heavy. I do feel like I have worked through so much of my grief in writing, and now that this is the last chapter, it is apropos to let them go.

I have one more tunnel I want to share before I wrap this up. For as long as I can remember, when you go through a tunnel, you are supposed to hold your breath and make a wish. I did, and after my family passed, my wish was for health, wealth, abundance, and love. When I got my dog King, I found my heart is filled with love, and one day while driving through a tunnel, I realized, *I have it all. I have my health. I have wealth.*

I have abundance. And I have love in my heart. I am so grateful for all the wonderful gifts I have been given in my life. My family is waiting for me on the other side when I am ready. I am not ready. I feel like I have a lot of living to do! So, they will have to wait.

I will strive to keep finding and living moments like this one. Such moments add value to my life and keep my spirit alive and soaring. When life happens, I will remember to deal and feel in order to heal, and I will go on and continue to live a charmed life....

ABOUT THE AUTHOR

Linda Blue is an author, keynote speaker, professional photographer, and survivor. Despite indescribable heartbreak and loss, Linda has always found ways to laugh, love, and share her kooky sense of humor with others. A resolute optimist guided by the angels of the ones she's lost, Linda turned to her personal journals to ask the hard questions about life. Inspired to help others with the answers she found, she wrote *Living a Charmed Life*. Today, Linda lives in Central California with her dog King.

BOOK LINDA BLUE TO SPEAK AT YOUR NEXT EVENT

When it comes to choosing an engaging speaker for your next event, Linda Blue is the perfect choice. Not only will she connect with your audience members on a human level, but she will leave them with courage to overcome obstacles and a renewed passion for life.

Whether your audience is 10 or 10,000, in North America or abroad, Linda can deliver a customized message of hope, healing, and inspiration for your meeting or conference. Linda understands your audience does not want to be lectured to, but rather understood, inspired, and given realistic steps to move forward with their goals and journey.

Topics Linda can speak to, depending on your audience's needs, include coping with the loss of loved ones, overcoming all kinds of loss from death and divorce to pets and failed dreams, the power of journaling for healing, and tips for writing your own inspirational memoir. Whatever your needs, Linda will rise to the occasion and deliver an impactful speech that will leave your audience wanting more.

Linda's speaking philosophy is to use humor and storytelling to entertain and inspire your audience. She will share her own amazing journey of grief and recovery, pain and renewed passion. Your audience will be left believing that if Linda can overcome her losses and still find joy in life, so can they. Help spread the hope by reaching out to Linda today.

To find out if Linda is available for your next meeting, contact her by text or email to schedule a complimentary pre-speech phone interview so she can better understand how she can help meet you and your audience's needs.

www.LindaAllenBlue.com

Linda@LindaAllenBlue.com

(805) 708-2583